The
100 Best
Things
I've
Sold on eBay

The

100 Best Things

I've

Sold on eBay

My Story

by The Queen of Auctions
Lynn Dralle

"It's a Numbers Game"

All Aboard, Inc.

Preface

This is not a how-to book for doing business on eBay. There are books like that, but this isn't one of them. This book is a collection of stories about some of the most memorable auctions I've been involved with on eBay. It does contain some tips and lessons for selling on eBay, but it is as much about me and my grandmother as it is about the world of online auctions.

Why is my grandmother such a big part of this book? There are lots of reasons. She's the one who got me started in the antiques and collectibles business, and she taught me most of what I know about antiques. It was because we needed to move a lot of inventory from her shop that I became interested in eBay in the first place. And eBay played a big role in my life during the time my grandmother was dying and I was learning to deal with that loss. For me, every story about eBay is also in some sense a story about my grandmother.

For the past five years, I've made a career out of eBay. In addition to buying and selling as a Power Seller on eBay, I've taught classes on how to run an eBay business, created an auction tracking system for eBayers (*iBuy* and *iSell*), written an eBay newsletter, and produced a couple of videos about making money through online auctions.

Last September while I was teaching one of my classes, I told the story about an Edwardian mourning case (see #74) that I'd sold earlier in the year. One of the women in the class yelled out, "That story gave me goosebumps!" My stories were her favorite part of the entire three-hour class. Wow! I realized that I had *lots* of stories to tell about my eBay successes (and failures).

I had been toying with the idea of writing a book about the 100 most important things I had learned from my grandmother. I had even started writing it, but it was slow going. Then, after hearing my student's "goosebumps" comment, I realized that I could combine both ideas into a single book. I could use my eBay experiences as a framework for my grandmother's story—the lessons she taught me, the stories she told, the life she lived. I was excited! Combining the two book ideas was a great way to make them both work. When I started writing *this* book I couldn't stop!

Now that you know what this book is about, I hope you enjoy reading it as much as I enjoyed writing it!

First Edition December 2003
Second Printing July 2004

ISBN: 0-9674404-6-7

For more information write:

All Aboard, Inc.
P.O. Box 14103
Palm Desert, CA 92255

AllAboard@mail.com
www.TheQueenofAuctions.com

Designed by: Lee Dralle, Becky Raney and Lynn Dralle
Edited by: Susan Thornberg

Printed in the United States of America
Print & Copy Factory
4055 Irongate Road
Bellingham, WA 98226
www.printcopyfactory.com

For my grandmother,
Cheryl Leaf

I miss you

1912-2000

Acknowledgments

The greatest thanks to:
Cheryl Leaf
Print & Copy Factory-Becky and Larry Raney
Lee Dralle
Susan Thornberg
Houston and Indiana
Sharon Chase
Wayne and Sue Dralle
Kristin Dralle
Melanie Souve
Peter James Gineris
Sally Huff
Maria Cota
Brianne Smith
Alexis Babcock
Grace Dexter
Melissa Schwartz
Audrey and John Mortensen
William Wilson
eBay
Jon Brunk Photography
My super Learning Annex students
AND all our great eBay customers!

Contents

Introduction

The 100 Best Things

Afterword

Introduction

My Grandmother

My grandmother, Cheryl Leaf, owned and operated her own antiques and gifts store in Washington State for 52 years. She was a well-known and highly respected dealer and a genius at business. She started bringing containers of antiques over from Europe in the 1960's, before other dealers thought of doing that. She taught me just about everything I know about antiques and collecting. She trusted me to work in her store from the time I was two years old. I was free labor! I learned a great deal from this amazing lady, not only about collecting, but also about working hard and having a positive outlook on life.

She started her shop in November of 1950 in an extra room at the front of her house on a temporary permit with the city. The business grew and grew, and soon it had taken over another room in the house. She had my grandfather, an architect, move a paneled wall every time she needed more space. And she needed more space all the time! Finally, the shop took up the entire living room and dining room, and in 1969, she decided to build an addition. The addition became her home (with a rental unit upstairs), and eventually the original house was used exclusively as shop space.

I grew up in Bellingham and worked for my grandma every summer and on weekends. We always had so much fun! After high school, I went to college in Los Angeles, but came home every summer to help her. I decided to stay in L.A. after college and lived there until 1993 when

The Bellingham Herald   March 29, 1971

KNOW YOUR ANTIQUES—Cheryl Leaf, Bellingham, who has been in the antique business 21 years, will give a presentation and display on antique reproductions to benefit the Whatcom Museum of History and Art restoration fund, at 7:30 p.m. Tuesday in Veroske's Chapel, 800 E. Sunset Drive. Mrs. Leaf, seen here with her 7-year-old granddaughter, Lynn Dralle, Monmouth, Ore., holds an antique mother of pearl satin glass while Lynn has an imitation. Lynn is a "junior student" of the subject. In front are old and new moustache cups. The speaker will explain how to tell fake or genuine articles. Tickets may be purchased at the door.—Herald photo.

my grandmother fell and broke her hip. She had survived breast cancer, lung cancer, and bone cancer over the years and was already in a wheelchair. I knew that going to a nursing home was going to be devastating to her, so I made a difficult decision. I decided my grandmother needed me more than L.A. did, and I moved back to Bellingham to run her business and keep her living in her home.

Antiques Business and the Internet

In the years after I returned to Bellingham, the antiques business changed dramatically. The advent of such TV shows as *Personal Fx* and *The Antiques Road Show* brought antiques and collectibles into the mainstream of American culture. The World Wide Web led to the growth of online antiques stores and online auctions, which altered the antiques marketplace.

The biggest change is that collectors no longer have to go from shop to shop to find that one elusive treasure. They can find what they are looking for from the comfort of their own home on the internet. Hitting the pavement to do an old-fashioned antiques treasure hunt is still a great pastime and the best way to find a "sleeper." My grandmother said that there is a "sleeper" (bargain) in every store if you are savvy enough to "smoke it out."

The internet has made this an exciting time for antiques dealers and the buying public. But entering the online world can also be scary and intimidating. Everyone has the choice of either ignoring the advent of the internet, or turning it into a great marketing (or buying) opportunity.

Our store started a web page in 1995. While we experienced great success with it initially, our online business slowed as the popularity of online auction sites like eBay started growing. Online auctions are simply easier for most collectors to use. On one auction site, they can find millions of items up for sale, and the auction format holds out the ever-present promise of getting a spectacular bargain. Instead of spending hours surfing the web, collectors have started spending hours surfing eBay.

I stayed away from eBay as long as I could. A friend of mine in town who had a consignment store was making a lot of money on eBay and kept encouraging me to try it. I think I was intimidated and didn't know where to start. I became an eBay registered member in September of 1998 but didn't really start selling until 1999 when it became clear that my grandmother would finally have to go into a nursing home. The time had finally come to jump on the eBay bandwagon.

We had an enormous amount of inventory—a shop, house, attic, basement, and garage full of wonderful merchandise—but not a lot of cash. Good nursing home care is expensive and was expected to run from $7,000 to $10,000 a month. One of my grandma's favorite sayings—and a line she became famous for—was, "If we don't have it, nobody needs it," and as we looked at all of her things, it seemed truer than ever. The easiest way to turn her inventory into cash quickly seemed to be eBay, so we decided to enter the world of online auctions.

A6—The Bellingham Herald Wednesday, November 1, 1995

BUSINESS

Antique shop runs on senior's savvy

MARKETS: Cheryl Leaf's dictum: 'If I don't have it, nobody needs it."

OLDER AND WISER: At age 94, there is little about antiques that Cheryl Leaf doesn't know.

Online Auctions·eBay

It took me about a week to list my first item on eBay. I read every book I could get my hands on and shopped for a digital camera. I think the shop bought and returned about six cameras before we decided on a little Cannon (I now use an HP 620 which was a Christmas gift and it is just great). Back when the shop started selling, one of the biggest challenges was setting up our own web site to host the photos, but luckily I had my computer-savvy brother to help us! (Today, eBay takes care of hosting photos for its sellers.) Finally, I was ready.

The first few things I sold on eBay brought in big bucks (See items #1, #2, and #3), and I was hooked. It was 1999 and we were known on eBay as LAWilson. Before I knew it, we were selling $20,000 worth of merchandise a month—more than enough to cover the nursing home expenses. We quickly became eBay Power Sellers at the silver level, which meant that we had over 98% positive feedback and we consistently sold over $10,000 a month. I was fortunate that my grandmother was able to see some of these successes. She would come to the store two days a week from the nursing home and help me identify things and price. Even when she couldn't speak anymore, she would nod her head to let me know what she thought. She was a fighter! When I would show her the auction screens and how much things had sold for, her eyes would grow really big. She loved to both buy and sell things. She was the ultimate retailer.

When I started selling on eBay, I also started buying. Auctions can become quite addictive. I got hooked on Texas Ware Melmac bowls from the 1950's, and within a few months I had a collection of more than a hundred. Boxes would come to me at the shop almost every day, and my sales girls were like, "What are you doing?" It was so much fun. In the comfort of my own home, I was able to find things that I had looked for in antique stores for years. One of the things I searched for regularly was "Marmorzellan" by Galluba and Hoffman. I had started a Marmorzellan collection at age twelve when my grandmother bought me my first piece, a gorgeous vase. She paid $13.50 for it ($15 less the antique dealer's 10% customary discount). We looked together over the years at antique shows and in antique stores for more pieces and we never found a one. Since I've started scouring online auctions, I've added five pieces to my collection. They mean a lot to me because of their connection to my grandma.

Because I was buying and selling so many items, I found I needed an efficient way to keep track of my sales and purchases. I just couldn't afford to accumulate any negative feedback by forgetting to ship an item to a paying customer or forgetting to pay for an item I'd won. In 1999, I created two loose-leaf binder systems named *iBuy* and *iSell* that I used to stay on top of my online transactions. I shipped them off to eBay corporate and a short time later got a phone call saying, "This is exactly what we have been looking for." eBay carried my books in their online store for three years. I felt honored.

Because of my eBay tracking system and my Power Seller status, I started getting requests to do radio interviews and television shows. The NBC affiliate in Seattle, KING TV, has a show called *Evening Magazine* which sent some people up to Bellingham to film me going to garage sales. I spent $31.50, and we saw it turn into $218.50 on eBay. I then did a national TV show, *The Rob Nelson Show*, on which I sold some items for my friend Grace who had just inherited a houseful from her aunt. Soon, people were calling me The Queen of Auctions. I changed our user ID in 2002, and now I sell under the name "TheQueenOfAuctions."

The TV shows were such a hit and received such enthusiastic responses that we did a video series, *Trash to Cash*, which showed how to find things to sell and how to sell them at online auction. In my video series, I show how 74 dollars' worth of garage sale purchases can turn into $569 in cyberspace.

With all this publicity, I was asked to teach a class on how to buy and sell on eBay for The Learning Annex in Los Angeles, San Diego and San Francisco. I taught about 50 classes over two and a half years. It was very rewarding and I hope that I helped some people change their lives and careers. I get a lot of nice email from former students sharing their success stories with me. One person whom I know I helped is my friend Roz in Texas. A single mom like me, Roz was able to quit her job as a flight attendant and now supports herself and her son by selling things online. Her career change has left her with a lot more time to spend with her son. She is my biggest fan!

Teaching the eBay classes was a growing experience for me. In college, I had to take a speech class to get my business degree. It terrified me to speak in front of people, so I did a semester in Spain and only had to speak in front of one person—my teacher! Even after teaching fifty classes, I still get a little nervous when I have to speak to a crowd, but I have definitely faced and overcome my fears. In the spring of 2003 I decided to stop teaching and focus on other things. The last class I taught was in September of 2003, and it was during that class that a woman yelled "I've got goosebumps" after hearing my Edwardian hair story (see #74). It dawned on me that I have enough wonderful tales to tell from all our experiences to fill a book! I have used these hundred-plus stories as examples in my classes so many times that this book nearly wrote itself.

Sadly, my grandmother passed away August 2, 2000. When she died, I lost my best friend and mentor. I miss her every day. It took us the entire two years following her death to settle the estate and liquidate most of the store merchandise and her personal items. We finally closed the retail location on August 2, 2002. There was still so much merchandise left that the four of us who inherited (my mom, my brother Lee, my sister Kristin and myself) divided up the remaining items to sell for ourselves on eBay. It really is a family business for us. My brother (user ID LDralle) and sister (user ID CaesarPalace) sell occasionally and I still do eBay full time. My mom (user ID TheXStyles) buys a lot on eBay and is a wealth of information on mid-century modern. The four of us are in constant contact with each other in order to share our newest eBay story or to get an "expert" opinion on an item.

After the store closed, I was able to move back to California in October of 2002 and continue doing eBay from my new home. The beauty of eBay is that you can literally do it from anywhere. We live in Palm Desert, which is beautiful, but extremely hot in July and August. So for those two months, I packed up my two children and headed up to my mom's house on the ocean in Bellingham. We had a great summer, and I was able to continue my eBay work from her home. The only problem was that she couldn't get digital internet access at her home and I was stuck with dial-up. It drove me crazy. I soon found that Kinko's offers free digital access if you have your own laptop, and I ended up spending a lot of time there. I referred to Kinko's as "my office."

The flexibility of selling on eBay is wonderful. However, I really miss having a shop to go to every day. My grandma's antique shop was everyone's home away from home. Friends and family would just drop by to say hello or have lunch with us. My kids would come over after school and do little jobs for me. It was a unique place full of energy and creativity. I would like to recreate that shop here in California. I plan to open a store soon—with an eBay division in back! Wish me luck.

Choosing The 100 Items

The 100 best items that I've sold on eBay are not simply the items that have sold for the most money or shown the greatest profit margins (although I've included a few of those). Instead, they are the ones that have great stories attached to them—the ones that are most likely to give you goosebumps (see item #16, about Lucky the Teddy Bear). Or the ones that just plain amaze you (yes, people actually buy match books—see #97). Or the ones that I used when teaching my classes to illustrate a key point (see #39, the quilt disaster). I also included some items simply because they helped me tell my story. We have probably sold 20,000 things on eBay. These are the first *Best 100*.

Just a note on the auction write-ups: I wanted to include some record of the price paid for each item, because I know that selling price doesn't mean much if there's no buying price to compare it to. But I didn't actually *buy* all of the items. The method we finally came up with for recording the original price of each item is that if the item came from my grandmother's personal collection or from the store and I was able to figure out how much it cost her originally, the write-up says, "Grandma paid..." or "Shop paid..." If I couldn't figure out the original price paid, the write-up records the price paid as $0.00. If the item was free, the write-up says "Free" (people actually do give things away—see Tole tray, #94). If the item was a gift to me, the write-up notes who the giver was and the fact that the item was a gift. If it was something that had been used (like my son's old clothing—see Gymboree Lot, #26) we put a "?" for price paid.

Last Words

As an ending note, please understand that selling on eBay is not easy. It is very labor-intensive, jackpots are few and far between, and most things sell in the $10 to $20 range. A lot of items will never bring in more than $1.99, and not everything will sell for even that much. I have to move a lot of merchandise to make a good living. I still make a lot of mistakes, even though I have been doing this my whole life! Every so often, I have to hold a "$1 sale" to get rid of everything that hasn't sold (think 99-cent store). These sales are very successful in liquidating the leftovers. The first one we ever had was at the shop in Bellingham, and the first day we sold $3,000 worth. Wow! I also donate things that don't sell to charity.

Because there are a lot of things that will never sell on eBay (and I still can't predict which ones they will be!), I try not to spend over $5 for any one item. When I am trying to decide whether or not to buy an item, I use a "ten times" rule. It's just not worth my time to cart something home, write it up, photograph it, answer questions about it and mail it out to the winning bidder unless it sells for ten times what I paid for it. Overall, I'm pretty successful at achieving that ten-fold return. If I go to garage sales on a Saturday and spend $100, I can be pretty confident that it will turn into $1,000 on eBay.

The world of online auctions is very strange. Selling on eBay really is a numbers game, and the more items you put up for auction, the bigger your chances of success. But I love the hunt, doing the research, remembering what my grandmother taught me, and counting my money! Good luck to you in your treasure chase!

The 100 Best Things

#1 U.S. Navy Plaque

$1.⁰⁰ **Paid**

From: Kiwanis Club sale
Bellingham, WA

USA Large Navy Tray MCMXLIII Plaque-Old-NEAT!

Description:
Really neat old tray or plaque has a hook on the back for hanging.
It is quite large, heavy and well made. About 20" in diameter. It
says "Navy Department United States of America" on it and has
a ship in the center. It is marked on the back with "MCMXLIII." If
anyone knows anything else about this tray, we would appreciate
knowing. In very good to excellent condition.

Winning Bid:

$51.⁰⁰

Ended: 5/2/99
History: 12 bids
Starting Bid: $1
Winner: Washington, D.C.

Viewed
000062 X

U.S. Navy Plaque #1

The Story

When I decided in early 1999 to test the eBay waters, I didn't want to start out with things from the shop. I wanted to go out and hunt for some unusual and unique items to see if what people were saying about eBay was true—that it could help turn trash into cash. My mom loves going to yard sales, so one Saturday in May I enlisted her help.

We knew we could improve our chances of finding valuable items if we took the time to map our route the night before. We went through the paper and circled the best sales first (these are usually the ones that say "estate," "lots of stuff," "miscellaneous," "community sale," "charity sale" and "multi-family"). We tried to pick key garage sales to be at exactly when they opened. On this particular day, there was a Kiwanis Club Charity Sale that started at 9 AM in an empty store in Bellingham. That would be the one we hit first.

We arrived right on time and were pleasantly surprised to find lots and lots of stuff and no other shoppers! No competition is always a good thing. There were some really neat things. I picked up this large metal tray for $1 and a covered Mexican

pottery hen for $2. I bought many other items that day but these were the two that stick out in my mind.

I took my time writing up those first few auction descriptions for eBay. At that point I wasn't up on my Roman numerals and had not taken the time to figure out what the date marked on the tray was. I should have called my librarian father to help me, but instead I asked for help from other eBayers in my listing. This is a trick that I use a lot and you won't believe how nicely and how quickly people respond. I think it was a day later that someone emailed me to say that the roman numerals stood for 1943, and this was in fact a piece from WWII. How cool was that! It was too late to change my listing because it already had quite a few bids.

The price on the tray went up quickly and on day three of my seven-day listing it was already at $38. It ended up selling for $51, and my hen went for $27.99. My grandmother always said, "Buy low, sell high." I decided eBay was for me!

#2 Chintz Side Teapot

$25.00
Paid

From:
Drop-in seller at the shop

RARE Ducal Purple Chintz TEAPOT w/side spout!

Description:
Wonderful purple chintz pattern is signed "Crown Ducal" and it is just lovely with purple, blue, green and rose being the main colors. Birds and other flowers make up the decoration. Vintage. This auction is for a very rare teapot with a side spout. In very good to excellent condition with no chips or cracks. Slight overall crazing which is common in older china. 6" by 4½".

Winning Bid: **$1,079.00**

Ended: 8/28/99
History: 37 bids
Starting Bid: $199
Winner: McLean, VA

Viewed
000578 X

Chintz Side Teapot #2

The Story

This teapot walked in through the front door of our antiques store in Bellingham, Washington, in 1999. Of course, someone was carrying it. My grandmother never went to garage sales for her merchandise, and she was very proud of that fact. She bought most of her items from other dealers or from people who brought things in to sell. Almost every day someone would come in to sell us something.

It was amazing to see my grandmother in action. She would never make an offer for an item. She was very savvy this way. One of her favorite sayings was, "Whoever names the price first loses," and she was right. In any negotiation it is much smarter to keep your mouth shut and let the other person throw out the first number. Also, she knew that if she made an offer, that person could then take the item all over town, saying "Well, Cheryl Leaf offered me $100, so how much will you give me?" She never wanted to be used in that manner. Once a price was named and the person was deciding whether or not to take it, she would say, "Once you walk out that door, the offer is not good anymore."

My grandmother was not doing the buying anymore when this item came in. The seller brought it in several times before she decided she could part with it and named her price. I didn't know much about chintz when I bought it, and it's really only because of this auction that I now realize how valuable certain chintz pieces are.

This was about 4½ years ago and I was still selling in the store and just starting on eBay. I decided to put this on eBay at a high starting price of $199. We began to get inquiries immediately. One very nice Canadian lady let us know that she found this shape in a chintz catalog and that it was dubbed a coffee pot. She felt that it was for strong coffee served with demitasse cups. She said that chintz collectors are a happy and crazy group and that if this was in her pattern, "Crown Ducal Ascot," she would bid in a minute and probably mortgage the house for it!

The term "chintz" refers to a layered floral design, and it's been popular for over two centuries. Chintz patterns started out on textiles. It wasn't until 1928 that a china company then called Grimwades (known since 1930 as Royal Winton) released their first chintz pattern, called "Marguerite," after the company's owner used his background as a lithographer to figure out how to transfer the brightly colored designs of Indian chintz fabric to china. Chintz went on to be made by many other factories over the years. It is highly collectible, as we came to find.

This was one of our first auctions that went really high, and I would wake up in the middle of the night to check the price. Okay, okay, I admit it—I was getting addicted. I just couldn't believe how high this piece went.

#3 1970's Skateboard Mags

$2.⁰⁰

William Paid

From: My ex-husband who had a subscription as a kid

SKATEBOARDER MAGAZINE-NOV 78-VOL 5, NO 4

Description:

This Skateboarder Magazine Vol. 5 No. 4 from November 1978 is in near mint condition with the exception of a missing centerfold. On the cover is Florida's Mike Folmer at Lakewood's Skateboard World (dig them Sims Snakes!). Issue includes original subscription form. This magazine has an article of particular historical significance on the evolution of the "Pig" (i.e. 10"+ wide deck) skateboard. It also includes great coverage of European skating, rollerskating on vert, Winchester Pro Bowl, and a Skate Tip on the invert by Bobby Valdez (see pic). Also includes full color ads for early Snowboard manufacturing attempts: the Snow Skate and the Skeeter (pic).

Winning Bid:

$107.⁰⁰/4

Ended: 11/16/99
History: 26 bids/4
Starting Bid: $9.99 each
Winner: Sacramento, CA

Viewed
`000125` X

1970's Skateboard Mags #3

The Story

When I saw how anything and everything was selling on eBay and bringing in big bucks, I decided that it was time to clean up our house and see what we had lying around to sell. It is amazing how many Americans are pack rats. You would be surprised what is in your own home to sell!

My ex-husband (well, he was my husband at the time) had been an Oregon State Skateboard champion when he was 12 years old. He had piles of old skateboard magazines from the 1970's. We thought we would give them a whirl on eBay. You can tell from the auction description that it was not written by me, but by a very knowledgeable skateboarder. It is very important to put as much information in your listing as you possibly can. Buyers on eBay will often search by both title and description, and because we included so much detail about the articles in the magazines, we got a lot more bids than we would have had we just listed the volume numbers. In fact, we started getting emails from some of the skateboarders actually featured in these articles, and we later discovered that these were the guys bidding.

Although I have just included one auction description in this story, we actually sold the four magazines we listed to the same man for a total of $107! The most expensive of the bunch went for $33. Who would have "thunk" it? My grandmother could not understand this auction. She always said, "If it is junk when it is made, it will always be junk." She considered these junk, but boy did they sell!

#4 Kewpie Card Holders

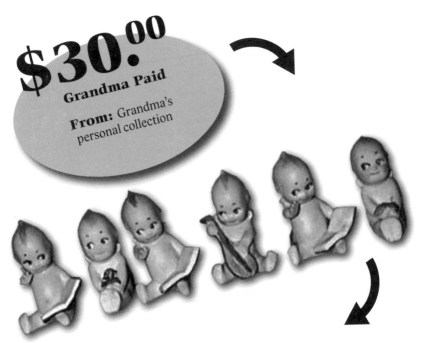

$30.00
Grandma Paid
From: Grandma's personal collection

6 Kewpie Doll Card Holders-Rose O'Neill-RARE!!

Description:
Amazing set of 6 authentic Rose O'Neill Kewpie Doll Bisque place card holders. There are 3 holding books which measure 2 1/8" by 1½". There are 2 holding flowers which measure 1 ¾" by 1½". There is one with a mandolin which measures 2" by 1 ¼". These are in very good to excellent condition. One of the card holders with the flowers has part of the rose broken off. 5 of them have the original paper labels which say Rose O'Neill on them. This comes directly from my grandmother's personal collection and is one of her most treasured items. Don't let this auction pass you by—an item like this comes along once in a lifetime!

Winning Bid: **$2,452.00**

Ended: 12/22/99
History: 18 bids
Starting Bid: $999
Winner: Defiance, OH

Viewed
000322 X

Kewpie Card Holders #4

The Story

I am always asked in my classes and in interviews—what is the most expensive thing that you have sold on eBay? It is a good question. With the advent of shows like *Antiques Road Show,* America is being shown items that appraise (not necessarily sell) for huge dollar amounts. In some senses, it has really hurt the antiques and collectibles business because now everyone thinks that their item is one of those $10,000 hidden treasures.

We thought that in all of my grandmother's collections and in over 50 years of being a dealer that she would have had at the very least one $10,000 item. While I was the executrix for the estate, I used to tease my family that I was still looking for that one-million-dollar item she had put away for us. We never found it, even though I was insisting it was there right up until we closed the doors for good. We came to realize that she had given away her most treasured items to us over the years and that they were already in our personal collections. She had so many cabinets of wonderful things in her home. When we would visit, she would say, "See something you like?—It's yours." She was such a gem!

These darling Kewpie Doll place card holders were our most expensive item. My grandmother collected authentic Rose O'Neill Kewpie Dolls and had a wonderful collection that she displayed in a cabinet on the wall in her bedroom. Rose O'Neill (1874-1944) was an amazing artist. She debuted her Kewpies in a 1909 Ladies Home Journal drawing and poem.

Shortly after that, she started making Kewpie doll figures in nine different sizes. Rose earned an estimated $1.4 million from the Kewpies. Eventually, the Kewpie franchise spread to a large variety of merchandise. Authentic Rose O'Neill dolls have a black "c" marked in a circle like a copyright symbol on them. It is also a bonus if they have the original paper label that says "Rose O'Neill."

These Kewpies sold for over $2,000 right before Christmas in 1999. We rushed to get them shipped by Christmas. The darling couple who bought them, Carol and Roger Herret, wrote:

Dear Lynn,

I truly do appreciate your extra effort to get our Kewpies to us by Christmas. We opened our box today and everything is perfect! You had wrapped it all beautifully, and we enjoyed unwrapping each and every one of the little guys! They are wonderful! I will have these forever until they are inherited by my children and grandchildren. I never seem to sell anything! (Grin!) Thank you again, Lynn. Hope you had as nice a Christmas as we did!

Goosebumps! When I couldn't find my photo for this book, Carol and her husband Roger, went out of their way to send me several! My grandmother would be proud to know that her treasured Kewpies found such a great home!

#5 Lenox Boehm Bird Plate

$10.00
Shop Paid
From: The Tank
Bought from Lenox in 1979

1979 Lenox Boehm Bird Plate-Golden Kinglet

Description:

Mint in Box 1979 Lenox Boehm Bird Plate is 10½" and comes with all the paperwork—certificate of authenticity etc. This year's plate features the Golden Crowned Kinglet bird.

Winning Bid:

$42.98

Ended: 5/18/00
History: 5 bids
Starting Bid: $9.99
Winner: Salisbury, NC

Viewed

000048 X

Lenox Boehm Bird Plate #5

The Story

My grandmother made a fortune on collector's plates in the 1970's. They were all the rage—think Beanie Babies. She built a huge addition onto her original shop building with some of the money. In this new edition she put a fireproof room in the basement—it was a huge 15' by 20' space that we called the Tank. The collector's plates lived in the Tank. It was really a creepy place. One summer she had me work down there organizing the plates. I was 12 years old and made 75 cents an hour. I worked 100 hours and made enough for one-half of my 10-speed bicycle. I learned a good work ethic the old fashioned way.

When I moved back to Bellingham in 1993 from Los Angeles to help run her business I was faced with liquidating the remaining 10,000 collector's plates. WOW! I had already made a good dent when eBay came along and the online auction world really speeded up my mission.

This Lenox plate was one of many collectors plates we sold on eBay. It stands out in my mind, though, because I got to sell it twice after the first lady who bought it realized she didn't need it. Here is her email:

Lynn, I am sending you a check for $42.98. However, I don't want the plate. I have been bidding on the 1979 plates to give my four daughters. When I counted my plates the other day, I have enough. So enjoy your bonus!! Cordially, Betty

I wrote back:
Betty, thanks for the nice offer, but why don't you just pay me our eBay fees and I can relist the plate. Thanks, Lynn

She responded:
That is very nice of you, but I have already written the check. It will teach me to pay closer attention and not bid in the middle of the night! Have a good day. Betty

My grandmother always told me "Never look a gift horse in the mouth." She probably heard this from her father who was a farmer in Illinois in the 1880's. You can tell a horse's age by counting its teeth. Checking the mouth of a horse someone had given you as a gift in order to see how old it was would be impolite. So I took my grandma's advice, accepted Betty's offer, and relisted the plate. It sold for $52 the second time around, making the total price for the plate almost $95. eBay is really one of the strangest places on earth.

#6 Wee Folk

$2.00
Paid

From: Garage sale
Bellingham, WA

Wee Forest Folk Mouse Knitting Figurine-CUTE!

Description:
Darling little mouse figurine is marked Wee Forest Folk and is about 1½" tall. It is of a mouse knitting. In very good to excellent condition.

Winning Bid: **$217.50**

Ended: 5/29/00
History: 15 bids
Starting Bid: $9.99
Winner: Las Vegas, NV

Viewed
 X

Wee Folk #6

The Story

At garage sales you can tell who is buying for resale by watching them to see if they turn over items looking for signatures. I am the worst at this. It is so ingrained in my brain to turn things over that when I go to friends' homes I find myself looking for signatures. Several years ago, I was at my good friend DK's parents' house, and in their bathroom they had what looked like Hummel figurines. Of course I turned them over for verification and then I said to his parents Pat and Jerry, "What are you doing keeping your good Hummel figurines in the bathroom? They could get broken!"

If I go to a new restaurant with my family, they all shake their heads as they watch me check to see what brand of china we are eating on. I have to be very careful when I do this because I usually spill. It is an incurable habit.

I turned over this figurine at a garage sale and it was marked with the brand name "Wee Forest Folk." I had never heard of this name before but it sounded interesting, so I thought I would give it a try.

I got it home and did my research. I sat at my computer and did a search of completed auctions on eBay that contained the phrase "Wee Forest Folk." eBay makes records of everything that has sold in the previous two weeks available as public information. Searching completed auctions is a great way to do research on pricing, because you see what items actually sold for—not what they were listed for, and not what the bid is mid-auction.

With the figurine sitting on my desk, I sorted all the completed "Wee Forest Folk" auctions by "highest price" and found that these figurines could sell into the thousands of dollars. I was shocked! I discovered that "Wee Forest Folk" even has its own category on eBay.

Wee Forest Folk® is a small family business located in Carlisle, Massachusetts, which produces a line of miniatures, most of which are mice. The first "Forest Folk" was made over 30 years ago, and now the company's products have a huge following.

This one turned out to be "M-59 Pearl Knit Mouse," and it was made in 1981 and retired in 1985. Suggested price on the secondary market today is $350. Who knew? It turned out that this mouse did fetch a good price—over $200. That's the markup I like—100 times what I pay. A jackpot like this happens occasionally, but I usually make a return in the ten-times range. I love selling on eBay because I learn new things every day.

#7 Travel Ivory Chess Set

$10.00
Shop Paid
From: Shop
Marked $39.50

Antique Travel Chess Set-Wood Box-Ivory?

Description:
Super antique ivory? Traveling chess set with board comes in the original wooden box. The box is 6 7/8" by 6 7/8" by 1½". It is light and dark brown in color. The playing pieces are red and white in color. We don't know if they are ivory or not. They seem to have some cross hatches but it is hard to tell. This set is in very good condition. There are some scratches and dust. We date this piece to the 1900's.

Winning Bid: **$316.00**

Ended: 8/25/00
History: 28 bids
Starting Bid: $49.99
Winner: Miami, FL

Viewed

000158 X

Travel Ivory Chess Set #7

The Story

This little travel chess set had sat in the store for nearly 40 years. I rescued it from one of the lower shelves in our men's section and decided to give it a try on eBay. It was priced in my grandmother's handwriting at $39.50 and was covered with dust. I once asked my grandmother how she decided what to price her things and she said, "P.F.A." I said, "What?" She said "Pulled From Air." We laughed. I think what she meant was that it was an educated guess.

This is one of my favorite stories because it shows that a worldwide marketplace can change your business overnight. The chance of something this specialized selling in a shop in a tiny town was very small compared to the chance that it would find a buyer in the global eBay community.

I didn't know if the white pieces were ivory or not, so I said that in my listing. My brother, who is a Gemological Institute of America-certified jeweler, was living in Los Angeles at that time and couldn't test it for me. I decided to start the auction at $49.99 instead of my usual $9.99. Sometimes if you start an auction at too low a price, your customers will have doubts about the quality of the item and decide not to bid. Pricing is a tricky business (remember "P.F.A."), and auction starting bids are no different.

Immediately we had a lot of inquiries about this piece. Lo and behold, it turned out that there is a huge following for travel chess sets. They are quite a serious bunch of collectors. The lady who eventually won this auction also bid and won another larger chess set that we had up for auction.

Not in my wildest dreams would I have imagined that this piece would sell for over $300. There it had sat, day in and day out, in my grandmother's store in Bellingham for 40 years! It reminds me of the children's story *The Tangerine Bear*, about a little bear who sat in a store for years and years, always wanting to find a family to love him. Our little travel ivory chess set had finally found a home.

#8 Byers' Choice Scrooge

$9.00 Paid

From: Estate sale Bellingham, WA

Scrooge Caroler Byers' Choice Doll 1987-88

Description:
Byers' Choice Caroler Doll is the Scrooge. He is 13 1/2" tall and looks to be in excellent condition. He has the original Byers' choice gold label on the base. I am guessing that this is from 1987-88 and is retired.

Winning Bid: $659.73

Ended: 9/7/00
History: 32 bids
Starting Bid: $9.99
Winner: W. Brookfield, MA

Viewed
 X

Byers' Choice Scrooge   #8

The Story

I bought this caroler doll from an estate for $9. I knew that Byers' Choice caroler dolls were pretty collectible because my good friend Hank's family owns Jacob Maarse Florist in Pasadena, CA and they carry them in their store. Byers' Choice is a family-run business in Pennsylvania that was started by Joyce Byers in the late 1960's as a hobby when she couldn't find quality Christmas decorations. All the carolers are hand-crafted here in the United States by a team of artisans.

I checked on eBay for this particular Scrooge and found that he was probably from 1987 to 1988 and that they usually sold in the $20 range. I put him up for auction without much information. I started him at $9.99. Within an hour of putting him on eBay I got an email asking some very specific questions: 1. Are his hands made of cloth or are they clay? 2. Is the green base smooth or bumpy? 3. On the back of the figurine and on the top of the base is there any writing in black marker saying Byers' 84 or some other year?

I answered the email quickly. The hands were made of clay (who knew that this was important?), the base was bumpy, and there was writing on the back side in black marker that I had missed. Me who turns everything over and looks everywhere for signatures had missed this because I thought the gold foil sticker was it! It said "Byers' 83." I ended up emailing this same information to quite a few eBayers. I couldn't go in and change the listing because it already had bids. In fact it went up to over $200 in the first two hours. This was a great auction to watch. This one would wake me up in the middle of the night to check on it. I would call my brother and say—"Oh my gosh, check out Scrooge today!" It was a lot of fun to watch the progress!

The buyer, Jim, bought Scrooge for his wife, Lynn, who had recently retired from teaching. "A Christmas Carol" was her favorite story to teach. He emailed me and let me know that it was a rare 1st edition and is coveted by collectors because of the clay hands. They had all the other Dicken's series 1st editions and needed this one to complete their collection. Jim and his wife Lynn still have Scrooge behind glass; they were very helpful and sent me the photo we used in the book. Scrooge ended up selling for close to $700 because it had clay hands! My grandmother always said, "You make your money when you buy and not when you sell." She was right; I had bought conservatively and it paid off. I was in shock.

Jacob Maarse
Florists

#9 Bakelite Bunny Rings

$20.00 Paid
From: Estate sale Bellingham, WA

Pair Bakelite Bunny Rabbit Napkin Rings-CUTE!

Description:
Vintage and darling bakelite bunny rabbit napkin rings are 2 1/8" tall and 1/2" thick. The ring hole is 1 3/8". They are in excellent condition and one is depression green and one is yellow.

Winning Bid: **$132.50**

Ended: 10/1/00
History: 15 bids
Starting Bid: $9.99, $99 Reserve
Winner: Tacoma, WA

Viewed

000184 X

The Story

I was sitting in my office at the back of the shop one day when I got a call from Eric, a producer at NBC's *Evening Magazine* in Seattle. He had heard of me and wanted to do a show about eBay. He wanted me to pitch him an idea for an attention-grabbing show. I suggested that he send a camera crew to Bellingham and they could follow me around going to garage sales. We could put our best items up for auction and see how they did. He liked the idea! Two days later, reporter Mimi Gan showed up at the shop on a Saturday morning.

My good friend Audrey Mortensen was a trooper and went with me. Audrey was my first employee and worked at the shop for over eight years. We found quite a few neat things that morning and it was fun being filmed. We went back to the shop and I did my research and listed three items: a Wales adding machine, a Sears starburst clock, and these Bakelite bunny napkin rings. I paid $7 for the adding machine, $4 for the clock and $20 for the napkin rings.

Bakelite and Catalin are forms of phenol formaldehyde, a plastic, invented in 1908 by L.H. Baekland. There were two major types, cast and molded. Bakelite is molded, usually dark in color, and used for utilitarian pieces. Catalin is cast and used mostly for jewelry and novelties. Pieces in both types of plastic were popular from 1930 to 1950. These bunny rings were probably Catalin, but "Bakelite" is a much more common term. A random check on eBay reveals 5477 items listed with "Bakelite" in the title and only 183 with "Catalin." Which term would you have used?

To find out if a piece is Bakelite or Catalin, try this easy test. Hold the edge of the piece under hot running tap water for up to 30 seconds and then smell it. If it's Bakelite or Catalin, it will give off a phenol, or fresh shellac, odor.

The Wales adding machine sold for $50 to a man in England. The clock went for $36 and the napkin rings for $132.50 to Sherree in Tacoma, WA, of all places. When I emailed Sherree to ask if she had a photo I could use, she wanted to know why the napkin rings were one of my favorite items sold. I told her it was because they had been featured on *Evening Magazine.* She couldn't believe that she had missed seeing it. I told her I would make a copy of the show to send her. What a small world!

The show was a big hit and they aired my segment about eight times over two years. I became infamous in my little hometown.

#10 Kobako Mini Perfume

$1.⁰⁰

Shop Paid

From: The Snake Pit

Kobako Bourjois Mini Perfume Bottle—Beautiful!

Description:
Darling miniature perfume bottle is 2 1/2" by 1 3/4". It has the original gold foil label which reads "Kobako Bourjois." It has a screw top and still has some of the original perfume. It has a raised floral pattern and is just lovely. I think it is antique and would date to the 1930's or so. In excellent condition.

Winning Bid: $278.⁰⁰

Ended: 10/26/00
History: 24 bids
Starting Bid: $9.99
Winner: Northbrook, IL

Viewed
 000300 X

Kobako Mini Perfume #10

The Story

My grandmother never had enough space in her home, so she asked my grandfather, who was an architect, to build her a room off of their bedroom. It was about 8' by 15' and had floor-to-ceiling shelves on all four walls. There was a trapdoor in the floor and under the trapdoor was a 3-foot-tall cement crawl space that extended under the entire room. It was really creepy because the only way to get anything in or out of the space was by crawling under the floor. That is how the room got its name—the Snake Pit.

The Snake Pit was filled to the rafters with all sorts of treasures. My grandmother loved to buy, and if one was good, 100 were better. I was in there one day looking for stuff to put on eBay and I found a shoebox full of little perfume bottles. A few of them looked eBay-worthy and others were not. I priced the non-eBay ones and put them in the shop. One of the bottles was just beautiful, with an incredible raised pattern and some of the original perfume inside. I was going to put that one on for sure.

I did my research on completed auctions and nothing came up. I searched current auctions also, and there were no Kobako perfume bottles. Either it wasn't going to be worth anything or it was rare. That's the rub with doing your research—even if you don't find your item, it doesn't mean that it isn't worth trying.

My starting bid was only $9.99, and boy, did the bidding get going fast and furious for this little gem. It ended up selling for $278 and 300 people looked at the auction. Wild! Who would have thought a little empty perfume bottle would sell for so much?

We always include a newspaper article about my grandmother and the store in each box, along with a note of thanks. Customers really appreciate this little touch because the internet has really made shopping an impersonal experience. With eBay, almost all our business is done by email and my phone never rings anymore with a live customer on the other end. The woman who bought the perfume bottle sent us the nicest email:

Hello Lynn, Just to let you know, I received my Kobako mini today and I just love what I bought! Thanks for including the nice article about Cheryl Leaf and yourself! Hope we do business again! Loretta

#11 Marklin SK800 Locomotive

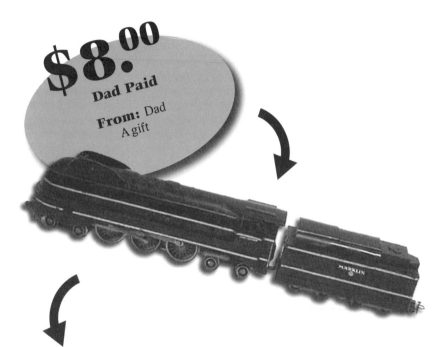

$8.00
Dad Paid
From: Dad
A gift

Marklin SK800 Locomotive-Tender-W Germany-OLD

Description:
We have a lot of vintage Marklin trains, cars, tracks and accessories up for auction this week. All were made in West Germany and many still have their original boxes. My father bought them from a man who had purchased them in Germany when he was there during the 1960's. All pieces are circa 1960. Many look like they were never used. This auction is for the Marklin SK800 Locomotive and Tender. They are in very good to excellent condition. This looks hardly used!

Winning Bid:

$457.00

Ended: 3/2/01
History: 30 bids
Starting Bid: $99
Winner: Morristown, NJ

Viewed
 X

Marklin SK800 Locomotive #11

The Story

When we moved to Monmouth, Oregon, in 1969 for my Dad to teach at OCE (Oregon College of Education), we bought a house on Sacre Lane. The man my parents bought the home from was an oil engineer who had been working in the Middle East in the 1960's. He took his two sons on vacation to Germany and they purchased an incredible number of Marklin trains, tracks and accessories. They were all in the garage of the house we were buying, so my Dad made a deal to buy the huge layout and all the extra boxes of trains. He paid $70.

He didn't tell my brother and I that he had purchased the set, and we spent hours in the garage moving wires, changing track and just generally messing it up. Then my Dad told us that it belonged to us now, and we were like "Oops!" Anyway, we never did get any of it running and 30-some years later my Dad offered to give me the boxes of trains to sell on eBay for my kids' college fund. How nice is my Dad?

The only problem was that my son, four years old at the time, was train crazy. He did *not* want me to sell the Marklin items. He did not need any collector's quality trains at his age, and he already owned so much Thomas the Tank Engine (which was age-appropriate) that he could have

laid track from Bellingham to New York. But we all have the collecting bug and my son is no exception. It was quite a battle to get the trains sold, but I managed to keep him away from the shop for about two weeks to get it all accomplished.

Marklin began in 1859 in Germany as a company that produced lacquered tinplated dollhouse accessories. They eventually got into the train business in the 1890's with one of the first layout systems. The Marklin system was popular because it could be added to piece by piece, and it was standardized. Marklin is known for finding the middle road between cheap mechanical mass production and costly hand-made production by craftsman. These trains are highly collectible and sought after.

I sold the items in about 50 different auctions. I was able to raise about $2,200 for my children's college fund. The item that sold for the most money was the SK800 Locomotive and Tender at $457. It was a beauty and went to New Jersey. The rest of the trains, track, cars and accessories went all over the world. We had buyers in the United States, Australia, Denmark and Portugal. eBay really is a worldwide marketplace, and the world is going to help send my children to college!

#12 Scary Butler

$150.⁰⁰
Shop Paid
From: Dept. 56

SCARY-Dept 56-Life Size GRAVELY the BUTLER!

Description:

Scare your friends to death!!! Have Gravely the Butler greet them at the door. He is the scariest, ugliest thing you've ever seen!!! He stand 5½' tall and holds a tray for your "delights." He is made of fiberglass and is hollow (he has no back side). We purchased him brand new for our store and used him as display. He is in excellent condition except for a little dust. Department 56—Suggested Retail $300. Reserve is our wholesale cost. Breaks down for shipping.

Winning Bid: $205.⁰⁰

Ended: 5/21/01
History: 14 bids
Starting Bid: $99, $149 reserve
Winner: Plano, TX

Viewed
000325 X

The Story

I bought this big guy at the Seattle Gift Show from Department 56, a well-known vendor that we carried in the shop. I thought he would be really cool to use in our store for a Halloween display and eventually I wanted him for my own house to scare trick or treaters. Once we got him into the store, we discovered a problem—he scared everyone! We sold Beanie Babies and had kids coming through the store all the time, and Gravely left a lot of toddlers cowering in the corner saying, "Mommy, let's go NOW." He just wasn't good for business.

In addition, I often worked late at night all alone in the store, and when I came around the corner in the dark I would almost have a heart attack. He was pretty imposing. On top of that, my kids were petrified of him and I realized he was never going to come home with me. I tried to sell him in the store to no avail and then it dawned on me—I'll try eBay! Because he was so big, I had not even considered it, and then I realized that he had been shipped to us by UPS so it would not be a problem. The buyers always pay for the shipping anyway. What did I have to lose?

I put a hidden reserve on the big butler because I did not want to get less than I had paid to Department 56 for him. Suggested retail was $300, so he had cost me $150. That is where I set the reserve. We had a lot of inquiries, and Gravely sold for $55 more than my reserve. This scary guy now lives in Texas. I hope the state is big enough for him.

#13 Bisque Santa Claus

$5.00
Grandma Paid

From: Grandma's personal collection

Victorian Bisque Santa Opening His Bag-RARE!

Description:

Fabulous 1890's Victorian Bisque Santa Claus Figurine is 6½" tall and 3" wide. He is opening his bag and the bag portion could be used as a vase. This piece is in OK condition. He has at some time been broken and reglued around his head and shoulders—hard to tell at first glance. Nevertheless, he will make a great cabinet piece. We think that he is probably German. A rare and genuine antique! This wonderful piece comes from our grandmother's personal collection.

Winning Bid: **$331.00**

Ended: 5/29/01
History: 2 bids
Starting Bid: $49.99
Winner: Hillsboro, OR

Viewed
000095 X

Bisque Santa Claus #13

The Story

My grandmother loved Christmas and Santa Claus. She always made Christmas very special for us. One year, when I was working for the May Department Stores in L.A., I was not able to fly home for Christmas (a drawback of *real* retail). None of us had ever missed a Christmas with my grandma, so it was a big deal. My whole family delayed Christmas for two days until I could home to celebrate with them. It was really touching!

One of the ways my grandmother expressed her love of Christmas was, predictably, through a collection. She had about 26 bisque Christmas figurines. We got this Santa ready to put on eBay. My mom was listing him when she said, "Oh my gosh—he's been broken and repaired." We hadn't noticed because it was a good repair job and he was a little dirty. (30 years without being dusted had something to do with that.) I knew he wouldn't sell for much because condition is everything on eBay. We decided to put him on anyway for $49.99.

We immediately got an email from Mary Morrison, who wrote:

I am very interested in your Santa, but do you guarantee that the piece is old? I have not seen this pose before. May I return it if in my own judgment it is not old? I have published a book on German Bisque.

I answered:

Mary, This piece has been on a shelf in my grandmother's home for many years. I do think it is old but I am not an expert. I don't think my grandmother would have gone to such an effort to fix him if he were a reproduction. It does have a "70" hand-painted on the base in the same red/orange as his suit. That marking is typical of older pieces. However, if he isn't old we will take him back. Thanks! Lynn

Mary did end up buying the Santa for $331 and we shipped him off to her in Oregon. I held my breath waiting to see if he really was antique. Here is her email:

Hello Lynn, My Santa has arrived and it is all I had hoped for! It certainly is old and probably German. We will be so glad to have this rare piece to include in our next book. Thank you for giving me the confidence to bid. Mary

I emailed Mary to get a photo for this book, and here is her reply:

Lynn, I do have your (well, now my) wonderful Santa and it will appear in my new book, *Mary Morrison's Big Book of Snow Babies* which can be found at www.marymorrison.org. We have pictures of it and will be happy to let you use one. Good luck with your book! Mary.

Goosebumps. I have already bought a copy. Wow! My grandmother would have loved to know all this! There goes my rule that condition is everything on eBay, and here is my new rule: "The exception is the rule on eBay."

#14 Kewpie Doll Arms

$2.50
Grandma Paid
From: Grandma's dresser

5 Rose O'Neill Kewpie Arms-Bisque-Doll Parts!

Description:
5 Rose O'Neill Kewpie bisque doll arms are 1 ¼" to 1 ¾" in length. They are marked 0, 4/0, 3/0 and the pair (one of the pair is marked 5/0). These arms are in very good condition. The fingers don't have any chips. These doll parts come from our grandmother's personal collection.

Winning Bid: **$122.55**

Ended: 6/10/01
History: 13 bids
Starting Bid: $24.99
Winner: Ft. Worth, TX

Viewed
000135 X

The Story

The Kewpie doll collection that my grandmother had was displayed in her bedroom in a wall shelf with a glass door. Underneath the shelf was a dresser. I found these Kewpie doll arms in a dresser drawer with other dolls in need of repair. You must keep in mind that my grandmother was the ultimate antiques dealer and didn't keep clothes in her dresser like most normal people—instead, she kept treasures!

I had been finding that sometimes parts would sell for more than a whole item on eBay. For example, in Victorian times, bride's baskets were all the rage as wedding gifts. A bride's basket was made up of a silverplated or sterling frame and a lovely glass bowl. I had tried several complete bride's baskets on eBay and couldn't get $99 for them. I lowered them to $49.99 and sometimes they would sell.

At the top of the Snake Pit I found five boxes full of just the frames. I didn't think much of them based on the fact that I could barely get $50 for a complete 1890's piece. I decided to try a few anyway. I couldn't believe it, but several of the silverplated frames sold for over $100. The highest went for $151! I guess there was someone out there who had the original bowl—probably a family piece—but desperately needed that particular size frame. Crazy!

Because of my success with the silverplated frames, I thought the doll arms would also have a good chance of selling. I knew that they were authentic Rose O'Neill arms because of the numbers on them. I checked the arms on other Kewpie Dolls with original labels that we owned and they had the same numbering system. These numbers are in the auction description.

I tried them at a high starting bid of $24.99 and couldn't believe it when they sold for $122.55. I have emailed the winner to see what she did with them but have not heard back. Hopefully, they are now attached to a warm doll body.

Kay just emailed me from Ft. Worth, Texas with a photo. Three of the arms are still unattached, but the other two now belong to a warm and darling Kewpie Doll!

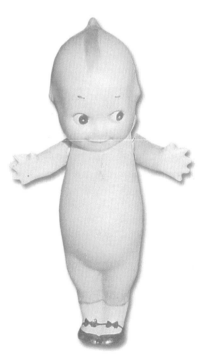

#15 Eskimo Doll

$4.00
Grandma Paid
From: The attic

Handmade Antique Eskimo Doll-Fur-Ivory Face!

Description:
Wonderful Eskimo (Native American) doll is 11" high. It is handmade and may have an ivory face. It looks like ivory to us. It is wearing a traditional real fur outfit. We date it to the 1930's to 1940's. This nice piece comes from our grandmother's attic.

Winning Bid: $104.50

Ended: 6/17/01
History: 2 bids
Starting Bid: $24.99
Winner: Northridge, CA

Viewed

Eskimo Doll #15

The Story

The attic was full also. Can you even imagine someone like my grandmother living and operating a store in the same house for over 50 years? I was overwhelmed by being in charge of the estate, especially because I had lost my grandmother and decided to get a divorce all within the same month.

To ease the pressure, I hired a wonderful lady from Bellingham to help me liquidate. Her name is Theresa Meurs and she owns a company called "Treasure Sales & Services." She used the upstairs apartment to hold estate sales and I would go through and pick out anything that I thought would sell better on eBay.

There were two ways into the attic: through a short fat door in the upstairs apartment, and up a pull-down staircase in the shop. It always felt like I was entering a wonderland when I went into the attic as a child. It was still a magical place for my kids—aged five and three at that point—and they were always begging to go up into it. One day when they were visiting the attic this darling little Eskimo poked his head out and I decided to try him on eBay.

I thought he was worth at least $49.99, so I put him on eBay for that amount. Timing and price were wrong because the auction ended with no bidders. I waited a few weeks and tried him again at a lower starting price of $24.99. Guess what? Two people got interested and that was all it took for him to sell for more than my original estimate. I got $104.50 for this guy!

This story really illustrates that timing and pricing have a great deal to do with whether your item sells and for how much. It also shows that all you need is two people who want your item to get the price up.

I just received a phone call from Sherman, the man who bought this doll. He has a collection of 75 Eskimo dolls now and he began collecting them after he honeymooned in Alaska. From our magical attic in Bellingham, WA to Northridge, CA, all because of eBay.

#16 All American Bear

$1.00
Grandma Paid
From: England 1960

Antique Mohair Teddy Bear-Fixer Upper-English

Description:
This darling antique mohair teddy bear is in need of repair. My grandmother purchased him in England in the 1960's. He is 12" tall and is missing an ear, both arms and one leg. His face needs help also. Once repaired he will be a special addition to any collection. All he needs is some TLC. Antique—we would date him to the 1920's or 1930's.

Winning Bid:

$24.99

Ended: 9/1/01
History: 1 bid
Starting Bid: $24.99
Winner: Jasper, IN

Viewed
000068 X

All American Bear #16

The Story

This auction revolves around a little mohair bear in desperate need of repair. My grandmother had bought this little bear in England in the 1960's. He was missing a leg and both arms and didn't have a face. He wasn't much to look at but my grandmother thought he was something special. I found him in the same dresser where I had gotten the Kewpie doll arms. This little bear had been there for over 40 years waiting for someone to fix him.

I found him shortly after my grandmother passed away and decided the best place to sell him would be at on-line auction. My mother didn't think we had a chance of selling this little guy but she agreed to try him anyway. We took his photo and wrote our listing based around a fixer-upper angle. To our surprise, he sold for $24.99. The lady who bought him was a really neat person. She sent us a thank-you card, pictures, and a note about how she repaired him.

Hello!   Sept. 20, 2001
Not long ago I won an auction for a little antique mohair teddy bear that had one leg, no arms, no eyes or facial features and one ear. When I viewed this little guy my first thought was that I could fix him. Well, as the pictures show, the operation was a success! Beneath that little sweater and pants, he now has all limbs replaced. By following the lines on his face, I carefully replaced his nose, mouth and eyes.

The reason that I am writing is to thank you from the bottom of my heart for making him available. I couldn't love him more if he cost thousands of dollars instead of $32.99 (including postage!). I named him "Lucky" for many reasons, but mainly because he was on the last flight before the shut-down on September 11th. Thank you very much for the most treasured bear of my bear family! Sincerely, Ginny & Lucky Jasper, Indiana

My grandmother would have loved this story, especially considering the fact that one of her favorite sayings was, "I am 50% Swedish, 25% Scotch Irish, 25% English, and 100% American." That little English bear became the "All-American Bear" after 9/11!

#17 Scotty Dog Stopper

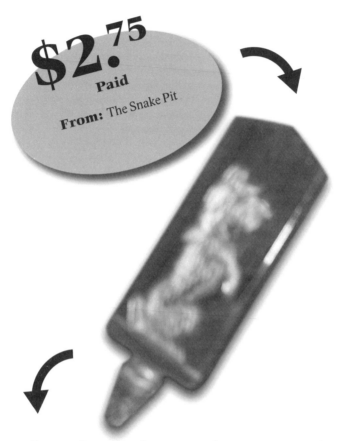

$2.⁷⁵
Paid
From: The Snake Pit

Scotty Dog Perfume Bottle Stopper-Red-Antique

Description:
Super antique perfume bottle stopper is red glass. It has an etched Scotty terrier dog in the center. This is a fantastic piece. 1900's or so. No chips or cracks. 4" by 1½". Rare and unique.

Winning Bid: **$128.**⁵⁹

Ended: 9/18/01
History: 13 bids
Starting Bid: $9.99
Winner: Kirkland, WA

Viewed
000102 X

Scotty Dog Stopper #17

The Story

Once again I was poking around in the Snake Pit and found about 13 shoeboxes full of stoppers. Just stoppers. My grandmother would buy stoppers by the apple box full all over the world. She never knew when she was going to get a beautiful perfume or cruet in need of a stopper.

We used to have so much fun trying to match them up. She called things like this "Indoor Sports for Light-headed People." We three grandchildren would carry box after box into her living room and we would try this one and then that one with a stopper-less bottle. When we found a fit, she would call it a "marriage." Then she would say, "Wasn't I smart to stockpile stoppers?" The stoppers were never for sale on their own. It was only after she passed away that I even dared to think of selling them.

Most of them were clear glass, but I found several boxes of colored-glass stoppers. One in particular caught my eye. It was red glass with—believe it or not—an etched Scotty dog in the center. Wow! Dog items sell really well on eBay. I had found a brass napkin holder with a bulldog on it in the shop when I first started selling on eBay. It had been marked $39.50 in the store, but when I put it on eBay it sold for over $150! Certain breeds of dogs have huge followings.

We put the stopper on eBay with a starting bid of $9.99. The bidding immediately started to go up quickly—$20, then $40. It was one of those auctions that kind of made you think, "Why?" Once again, the item was just a part of a larger whole—not complete in itself. It ended up selling for $128.59 to a really nice lady in Kirkland, WA. She sent me an email after she received it, saying:

> Lynn, the little Scotty arrived today in good condition and it is now in its own bottle which fits perfectly! Hope I can get to Bellingham soon!! Are you putting more stoppers on eBay? I've been watching! Rosie.

We did end up putting a lot more stoppers on eBay and were very successful selling them. Yes, my grandmother was smart for stockpiling those stoppers!

#18 Little Tikes Airplane

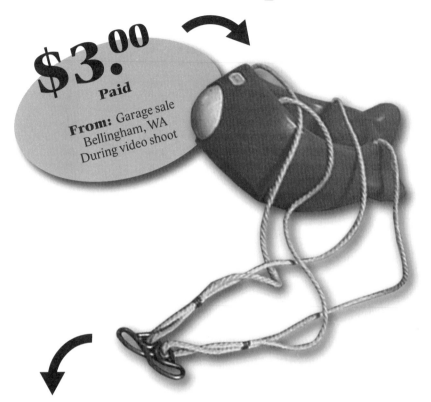

$3.00 Paid

From: Garage sale
Bellingham, WA
During video shoot

Little Tikes Red Airplane Swing-Classic-RARE!

Description:

Little Tikes Airplane is 26" by 16" by 14". It is red in color and is
marked with style number 4310-00 on the base. This was made for
children 9 months to 3 years. It is a classic toy and is rare because
it is no longer made. What a great gift for Christmas! This piece is
in very good to excellent condition. There are a few scrapes on the
nose and the seat belt is weathered.

Winning Bid:

$25.01

Ended: 10/30/01
History: 3 bids
Starting Bid: $9.99
Winner: Bellingham, WA

Viewed
`000028` X

Little Tikes Airplane #18

The Story

After the success of NBC-KING TV's *Evening Magazine* show I decided that creating a "How To" set of videos would be a great idea! My friend Audrey was married to a genius producer, John Mortensen. We sat down and discussed it, and in October of 2001 we started production. It was a blast and we got the videos done in about 2½ days of filming.

John and his crew followed me to Saturday morning garage sales. Bellingham is a small town, about 70,000 people, and when other garage-salers saw a camera crew following me, some of them recognized me. I could hear whispers of "That's the girl who has been on TV—she owns Cheryl Leaf Antiques. Go and see what she is buying." Some of them even went so far as to help me try and find things. It was really cute.

One of my favorite items was this Little Tikes airplane swing. I found it at a sale in a nearby condominium complex for $3. It was in really great condition. Little Tikes is a very popular children's toy company and it is pretty common to see this brand at garage sales. If they are in good condition, you can make a good return on them. When I got the airplane back to my house and did research, I found that it normally sold in the $25-to-$30 range. Not bad for a used kid's item!

The swing ended up selling to a woman in Bellingham, of all places. She had never been in the shop before and came in to pick it up, saving herself shipping in the process. This happened a lot. Our regular store customers were always checking our online auctions and would come in during the week before the auction would end and want to see something in person. It was really amazing how having an open store helped drive up the prices on a lot of pieces. When new customers would come in they would often say, "I've been driving by for years and never stopped. This place is amazing!"

#19 Apothecary Jar

$9.00
Paid

From: Garage sale
Bellingham, WA
During video shoot

Antique Drugstore Apothecary Jar Huge-RARE!!

Description:

Antique tall footed apothecary jar is 20½". These were used in drugstores for display in the 19th and 20th centuries. It is antique because it has a ground inside rim and the stopper is also ground. It is heavy and there are a few minor chips around the inside base of the stopper. I would date this piece to the 1890's. It has 15 thumbprints around the lid. The rest of the piece is in perfect condition. It needs a good cleaning.

Winning Bid: **$300.00**

Ended: 10/30/01
History: 12 bids
Starting Bid: $49.99
Winner: Independence, MO

Viewed
000278 X

Apothecary Jar #19

The Story

This was another piece that was featured on my video series, "Trash to Cash." I found this jar hiding in a corner at a garage sale on the south side of Bellingham. It was absolutely filthy and "him wants a wash" is what my grandmother would have said. I think that because it was so dirty it was only priced at $10, so I offered them $9 and they accepted. I knew it was a good piece because my grandmother had some similar to it in her personal collection—I just didn't know how good it was!

When I got it back to my house and did the research, I found that apothecary jars were used in drugstores and markets in the 1880's and early 1900's for display purposes. Pretty fancy display cases! I could tell that this was an old piece because the glass was ground on both the inside lip of the jar and on the stopper. Ground glass looks frosted and rough, not smooth. The number of thumbprints or indentations around the lid is important. From my completed auction research, I found that these jars sold in the $100-to-$300 range. Pretty awesome!

We put it up for auction along with the other items featured on the video. This auction was interesting because we filmed the last several minutes of bidding and watched the drama unfold. In the old days of online auctions, people would bid early and often. This would help drive the prices up. People had more time to react when they got that email that said, "You have been outbid." Nowadays, most auction shoppers wait until the final minutes or even seconds of an auction to bid. They don't show their hands and allow other bidders time to make the decision to increase their maximum bids. This practice of lying in wait until the final moments of an auction is called "sniping." There is even sniping software that bidders can use if they can't be at the computer when the auction ends. In this case, sniping didn't seem to hurt the sales price of the jar—it actually may have helped it. We watched this auction go from $200 to $300 in the last ten seconds. It was very thrilling to watch!

#20 XXXX Sign

$1.00 Paid

From: Garage sale
Bellingham, WA
During video shoot

XXXX The Classic Aussie Lager Bar Mirror-BIG!

Description:
This Classic Aussie Lager XXXX Beer Bar Sign is very large. It is about 4 feet by 18 inches. It has a red frame. The mirror portion is in good condition. There are holes from nails on the frame portion and part of the wood is split. It is scratched and chipped. A vintage bar sign—hard to find.

Winning Bid:

$46.99

Ended: 10/31/01
History: 11 bids
Starting Bid: $.99
Winner: Gettysburg, PA

Viewed
 X

The Story

This was another of the items featured in my how-to-sell-on-eBay "Trash to Cash" video series. This is a great example of how selling on eBay is a numbers game. I had picked this mirror up at the last garage sale of the day and the gentleman had to convince me to buy it. It was only $1, but it was in terrible condition. I had gotten a lot of great things from him (including hog scrapers) and he had given me quite a few free things (such as some Budweiser plastic longhorns), so I agreed to buy this as-is sign.

I got it back to my house and it looked in even worse condition in my immaculate living room, where we were filming. My producer, John, had to convince me to put it on. I was going to pass on it and not waste my time for the video series. "All right, all right," I finally said. "I'll put it on." I started it at 99 cents. This was such a fun auction to watch because it went up right away. I was in shock and would call John and say, "Get a load of that XXXX sign." It turned into a bidding war between two people and the darn thing ended up selling for $46.99.

This just goes to show you that the more items you put on eBay, the better your chances of making real money. eBay is a numbers game, and often the things that I think will sell for a lot of money (like the antique quilt I bought for the video series) don't, and the things that you think will never sell (like the XXXX sign) go for close to $50!

I had a hunch that the two bidders were both college boys and when the winning bidder emailed me with his charge card I found I was right—at least about one of them. Here is what he said in his email:

> Please leave me positive feedback, I think I paid pretty damn quick...hehe. Throw in a bumper sticker if you have one, I love to advertise for fellow eBayers.

He was a nice kid, and you know, that bumper sticker is not a bad idea—I can see it now: "The Queen of Auctions Rules." We shipped the sign to Gettysburg College and I'll bet it still resides there. It's not the type of thing that you move to your first apartment after college—or is it?

The video set turned out great—I ended up buying $74 worth of stuff that sold for $569 on eBay! Not bad for a Saturday morning at garage sales and an afternoon listing things on eBay.

#21 Casino Royale LP

$0.07 Paid

From: Garage sale Bellingham, WA

Casino Royale LP/Record-James Bond 007-Tattoo!

Description:
Casino Royale LP Record Album 33 RPM. It is in very good condition with a girl covered in tattoos on the cover. Original Soundtrack to James Bond 007's CASINO ROYALE, released by Colgem (COMO-5005) in 1967. Music composed by Burt Bacharach. Back of cover has photos from the movie (including Bond girl Ursula Andress). Vinyl record in good condition with some slight scratches but nothing major. Original owner's name is written on back cover.

Winning Bid:

$31.00

Ended: 3/14/02
History: 8 bids
Starting Bid: $.99
Winner: Maumelle, AR

Viewed
000076 X

Casino Royale LP #21

The Story

As we were getting closer and closer to settling my grandmother's estate, I was selling more items that I found at garage sales on eBay. I got a big box of 65 LP's for $5 at a sale near my home. This album ended up costing me seven cents. With old records, condition is extremely important and albums still enclosed in the original plastic covering can sell quite high.

I liked the cover of this album a lot and put it on eBay using the tattoo angle in the title. I started a bunch of albums at 99 cents. Once again, it really is a numbers game because others that I put up the same day sold for a lot less. "Whipped Cream" by Herb Alpert sold for $3.24, and The Beach Boys' "Surfin' USA" sold for $12.17. As a side note, I recently put up about five early Barbra Streisand albums and couldn't get 99 cents for any of them. A girl in my very first eBay class in L.A. told me that she was making $1,000 a month selling her old DVD's, CD's, albums and videos on eBay. Who knew?

I have also bought records on eBay. I find that a lot of people are buying these old albums for the covers, so cover condition is an important issue. I loved the Partridge Family when I was a kid. I had a huge crush on David Cassidy—who didn't? I had all their albums on a shelf in my office but was missing the one with "Point Me in the Direction of Albuquerque,"

so I bought it on eBay for about $3. It was fun. I told this story in one of my Los Angeles classes and a guy came up to me afterwards and told me, "My family is best friends with Shirley Jones, and I grew up with David. I just saw him for dinner last week." What a weird world!

This "Casino Royale" album sold for $31 which was a great return on a 7-cent investment. I just heard from the purchaser of this album and it is a great story:

"Hi Lynn, The record is in Arkansas. I gave it to my dad. He is actually responsible for the record's value. He was listening to the record and noticed that it was recorded in a unique way. He sent a copy to his friend, Harry Pearson of NY, who has a magazine, "Absolute Sound" (a very high-line magazine read by people in the music industry). Harry concurred and published his findings, sky-rocketing the value of the record (stereo version). Harry sent a copy of the article to my dad with a thank-you note attached. I thought it was pretty cool. This record was the first item I purchased on eBay. My dad really appreciated the thought behind it and we are both happy. Thanks—Johnathan"

#22 BMW Performance Chip

$?.00
Paid
From: My old car

Motronic BMW Performance Chip-1988 325is

Description:
This high performance chip comes out of a BMW 325is 1988. It is
Motronic Bosch 0261 200173. It's in great shape and works. Made
in Germany BMW design performance chip and it was used in my
car for 3 years. BMW 4256510.

Winning
Bid:

$34.00

Ended: 9/6/02
History: 2 bids
Starting Bid: $24.99
Winner: Jaffrey, NH

Viewed
 000030 X

BMW Performance Chip #22

The Story

In 1992, my grandmother called me in California and said "Honey, I have an extra $7,000 for everyone and Lee [my brother] thought you should use yours to buy a new car." Wow! How awesome was my grandmother? Pretty awesome! I had a Jetta GL that I had bought new in 1985 and I could really use a new car. I had wanted a BMW since I was a kid and our neighbors, the Thornbergs, always drove them. One of their daughters, Susan, is my editor for this book!

I took my old Jetta and the $7,000 and went to the BMW dealership. I found a beautiful used 1998 white 325is with black leather interior in my price range. I was in love with that car. My grandmother got to see it and ride in it when I moved home the next year. Every time I would drive her in it (and I drove her in it a lot because she couldn't drive anymore), she would say, "This is a beautiful car," and I would say "Thank you, Grandma."

A two-door car was not practical for a mom with two little ones but I didn't want to sell it. I became even more attached to that car after my grandmother passed away. She had always said, "Keep your overhead low," and I would have driven that car forever. My grandparents had bought a blue Econoline van in 1963 that they drove to Indiana in order to see me the day I was born. My grandmother drove that van for 15 years until I begged her to get a new one! I hated that van, but as she always reminded me,

"It's all paid for." She finally bought a 1978 Chevy van right when I was learning to drive. We still have it, 25 years later. I think it is parked behind my sister's house.

I had driven my car for ten years when, in March of 2002, I was driving to see my friend Teresa Thornberg, another of the daughters of my neighbors. A lady ran a stop sign and hit me, and my car was totaled. I was devastated. I guess someone upstairs thought it was time I got a new car.

I had added a high-performance chip in 1999 that cost me $300, but boy, did it make that car go fast! I called my mechanic, Kim Fairchild, and asked him if I could pay him to go and get the chip out. He told me that most of the $300 was labor and it would cost too much again in labor for him to get it out. He was kind enough to explain how to remove it to my dad. My angel of a dad got it out the next day. I also took the original manuals.

I put the chip on eBay and sold it for $34 and I got $28 for the original manuals. My grandmother's mantra had been "Never throw anything away" and I was beginning to believe her!

#23 BMW Gauge Cluster

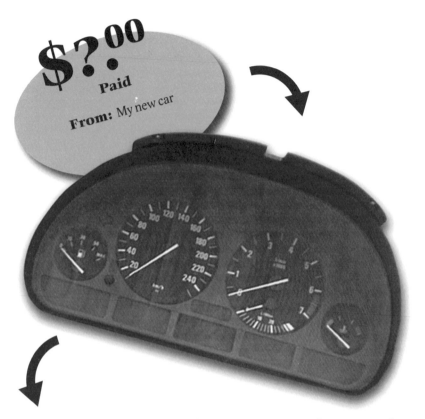

$?.00 Paid

From: My new car

BMW Odometer/Speedometer Gauge Cluster 528i

Description:
This speedometer gauge cluster comes out of a 1998 528i. It is metric and comes in its original box. It is an odometer/speedometer/fuel console which goes in the dash. Tachometer/temperature. It came out of a car I bought in Canada because I had to replace it with a US console. In excellent condition.

Winning Bid: $101.⁵⁶

Ended: 9/6/02
History: 2 bids
Starting Bid: $49.99
Winner: Philadelphia, PA

Viewed 000088 X

BMW Gauge Cluster #23

The Story

With my car totaled, I was forced to start looking for a new car. The timing was terrible because I had made the decision to move back to Southern California and I wanted to wait and buy a car there. The insurance company paid for a rental for a while so I had a little time. Of course, I wanted a car with four doors this time!

My mom had just bought a Honda minivan in Canada and had saved a ton of money with the exchange rate. I started looking online. I found three cars in my price range right across the border. I called my Dad and asked "Will you go up with me?" My Dad was my nanny and watched my kids during the day while I worked. Of course he said yes, and we went on a Monday when the shop was closed. We went to a BMW Dealership in Richmond, British Columbia, and I found the most perfect used four-door in "cashmere beige." I called my brother with the price and he looked it up online, checking the blue book values. He said that with the exchange rate it would be a great deal.

What put me over the edge was the fact that my grandmother had grown up in Cashmere, WA, and it was very dear to her heart. I had to have this car in the color cashmere! I got $7,000 from the insurance payout on my car but needed the balance in cash because you can't get a bank loan on a Canadian car. Strange that the payout on my car was exactly what my Grandmother had given me to buy it ten years earlier. I had to make it all work.

My wonderful mom and dad both came through with loans and I creatively financed the rest. I decided not to use a broker and saved about $1,000. This meant I had to drive it across the border myself and pay duty. I also had to get the odometer/speedometer cluster changed from metric to US. The new cluster was $1,000. The day I picked up that car and drove it home was an incredible day for me. I had a BEAUTIFUL car that was ten years newer than my former car. I could not wipe the smile off my face for about six months. As my grandmother used to say, "Someone upstairs must like me!"

I decided to sell the old metric cluster on eBay and I got $101.56. Who would have thought you could sell old car parts? I have heard great success stories with car parts and this is one of them!

#24 Chic Chandelier

$?.00 **Paid**

From: My house remodel

European Prism Chandelier-Shabby Chic-OLD!

Description:
Shabby chic brass prism chandelier is 12" high and about 12" wide. It is in good to excellent condition but needs a cleaning. It is from the 1950's and has a stylized leaf pattern and 4 arm sections with 4 prisms hanging from each. There are 4 additional "branches" with 2 prisms each for a total of 28 prisms. Suspending from approximately 100" chain to the base. You could add 4 prisms to the base but looks great without them. Solid brass rewired and it works! See the matching sconce also up for auction.

Winning Bid: $71.00

Ended: 9/7/02
History: 6 bids
Starting Bid: $49.99
Winner: Sacramento, CA

Viewed  X

Chic Chandelier #24

The Story

I had bought a 1950's house in Edgemoor in 1998. Edgemoor was the neighborhood I grew up in and the houses were expensive because they were close to the water. I found a fixer-upper and worked on it while we lived in it. I redid the bathrooms, put in hardwood floors and completely repainted. It turned out great! I bought the Jacuzzi tub for the master bath and the hardwood floors on eBay (of course). I got a brand-new Kohler Jacuzzi tub for $873 and saved about $1,200. My contractor was totally impressed with my eBay skills!

We closed the doors of the shop for good in August of 2002. It was very, very sad. At least I had a lot to keep myself busy. My remodeled house had just sold and I was moving to Palm Desert, CA, on October 11th— in about a month. We had brought over my quarter of what was left at the shop to my home and I was frantically selling things on eBay so that I wouldn't have so much to move.

The moving companies I talked to all wanted 40 cents per pound to move me. It turned out that I moved with 80,000 pounds, so it would have cost me $32,000 if I had gone that route. My dad searched high and low for an alternative plan and found a local trucking company that would deliver a 53' semi truck to my new house for $2,200. Amazing! All we had to do was load and unload it.

One of the items I found when packing was a little prism light fixture that I had taken down from the master bath during the remodel. It was really cute, so we put it and the matching sconce on eBay. It was very "shabby chic" in feel so we put that in the title. In the old days on eBay, you could use "shabby chic" in the title and it did help to sell things. I just assumed it was a generic term, but there is actually a company called "Shabby Chic" and they don't want anyone to use their name in auction titles. So no more. We will have to think up our own new term. The chandelier sold for $71 and the matching sconce for $31! Don't throw anything away—ever!

#25 Watermelon Spoon

$0.00 Paid

From: Inheritance

Old Watermelon Sterling Spoon-Enamel-RARE!

Description:

Amazing and rare sterling antique spoon is 5½" long and 1 1/8" at the widest point. It is marked "Charles W. Crankshaw" with a lion, anchor and "G" for hallmarks along with sterling. It has an enamel watermelon in pink, green and white. 1880's to 1900's. A head/face of an African-American young boy is done in sterling. In excellent condition. One of my grandmother's favorite pieces from her personal collection.

Winning Bid: $470.00

Ended: 9/12/02
History: 22 bids
Starting Bid: $99
Winner: Yorktown Heights

Viewed
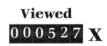 X

Watermelon Spoon #25

The Story

My grandmother always loved this piece. It was rare and special to her. I had gotten it as part of my inheritance and hated to sell it but I needed to raise a lot of money quickly. Even with the cheaper trucking company, the move was still going to cost a lot of money. I was also buying a home and needed to come up with some extra cash for closing costs. I had found my dream home in Palm Desert— 4,000 square feet, five bedrooms, five baths, a huge rec room to use as an office (keeping my overhead low), and a swimming pool. I had always wanted a house with a pool! My grandmother would have approved, so the little guy got put on eBay.

When I started looking this item up on eBay, I found that Black Americana items are very collectible and sell for quite a bit. Every item that you put on eBay has to be assigned to a category. I was surprised to find that there were quite a few categories for Black Americana collectibles. The category I finally chose was #29459:

"Collectibles – Cultures, Ethnicities – Black Americana – Housewares, Kitchenware." I thought he was worth in the $200 range after doing my research, so I started the auction at $99 with no reserve. It is scary starting an auction at a lot less than what an item is worth. Sometimes you just have to take the risk to get the bidding going.

Soon after I put this up for sale I received an email from a woman whose family had owned the Crankshaw Company, and she had some really great information for me. She agreed that it was in excellent condition and a very good example of their work. It never ceases to amaze me how nice the eBay community is! They will help you identify items whether you want them to or not. I love selling on eBay because I learn something new everyday and sometimes I even learn two things in one day! The spoon sold for $470! That was a good drop in my money collection bucket.

#26 Three Lots Boy's Clothing

$?.00 Paid

From: My son
His used clothing

13 pc Boys Lot 2-4T-Gymboree/POLO/Mickey-NICE
13 pc Boys Clothing Lot 3/4T-Gymboree-OUTFITS!
27 pc Boys LOT- 4-5T-Gymboree-Mickey-CUTE!

Description:

Boy's 13-piece lot is size 2-4 T. You get 4 darling outfits. There are even shoes included. Most is from Gymboree. All are in very good gently used condition. See our other auctions for more lots and save on shipping with multiple purchase. Outfit #1 is a yellow rain slicker, jeans, top, hat, socks, shoes all from Gymboree size 3T—includes shoes. Outfit #2 is a Dress Pant and red sweater set size 2T. Outfit #3 is Gymboree pants, shirt and my favorite orange jacket size 4T. Outfit #4 is Gymboree pants and zip sports shirt that coordinate with outfit #3 size 4T. Great LOT of little boy clothing!

Winning Bid:

$99.¹⁴/₃

Ended: 9/19/02
History: 30 bids/3 auctions
Starting Bid: $9.99 each lot
Winner: University Pl, WA

Viewed
 X

Three Lots Boy's Clothing   #26

The Story

I always bought my son the most darling outfits. He was my firstborn and Gymboree was my favorite store. When he turned 1½, my brother and I were working on a book on Beanie Babies that would become a best seller on Amazon.com. We wrote *The Book of Beanie Babies*, which was a loose-leaf system to keep track of which Beanies you owned and which you wanted to acquire. It was a great idea and sold extremely well. Scholastic saw it and commissioned us to write a book for them. We got a healthy advance and wrote *The Unauthorized Beanie Baby Guide* for them. It was a lot of fun!

For a while, I had a lot of discretionary income to spend at Gymboree. I became well known there! And my son always looked like a million (or at least a hundred) bucks. It was great until Ty Inc. decided to sue anyone who had ever written an unauthorized book about Beanie Babies. I learned a lot from that experience—like never sign for a registered letter, especially when you are pregnant.

My wild spending spree on children's clothing had come to an end. What did I have to show for all of this? Boxes and boxes of really small clothes. When I started packing to move, I realized I needed to part with some of these darling outfits. I wanted a way to show them to their full potential so I went on eBay and bought a little child's mannequin for $13.

We put each outfit on the mannequin to photograph it. I can still hear my friends, Alexis and Brianne, oohing and aahing over how cute the outfits were! Selling by the lot is the best way to go as far as clothing sales are concerned. The most expensive lot that we sold is the one featured here. It brought in $37.25! The winning bidder also bought another lot for $26 and another for $35.89. Overall, she spent $99.14 on my son's outgrown clothes, and those were just three of the auctions that I put up. I had at least another 20 auctions with some of my daughter's clothing also! Amazing how much you can get for used kid's clothes. I   dare you to try it!

#27 Marble Collection

$0.00 Paid

From: Inheritance

Grandmas Antique Marble Lot-150+ Swirls-NICE

Description:

This amazing LOT of marbles comes right from my grandmother's personal collection. She loved marbles and this auction is for 150+ marbles. They are in overall good condition for their age but a couple have a lot of chips. All date right around the 1900's and are hand made. There are 37 blue crockies ½" to ¾". There is one multi-colored crockie ¾". One large 1" dough baby. 65 Swirls ½" to 1". There is one large blue swirl shooter 1½". Three clear marbles ¾". 41 Brown crockies ½" to 1". One brown agate ¾". I am not a marble expert but did my best to describe. A great collection. Don't let it get away!

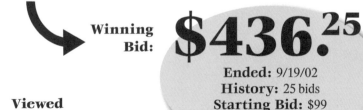

Winning Bid: **$436.25**

Ended: 9/19/02
History: 25 bids
Starting Bid: $99
Winner: Carlisle, PA

Viewed
000422 X

Marble Collection   #27

The Story

My grandmother had an amazing marble collection. She was a marble shooter from way back. She played a lot of marbles as a child growing up in Cashmere, Washington. She had huge glass jars full of her marble collection in her living room and she kept them on marble-top tables. Ironic. The marble-top tables were Victorian and really beautiful. She gave both of the tables to me and I have them in my living room today—I will never sell them.

Cheryl Leaf loved marbles so much that she acquired a Victorian 1880's cameo brooch that showed her two favorite things: angels playing marbles on a cloud. It was featured on the cover of a marble collector's publication. People from around the world would contact her about purchasing this cameo brooch. She would not sell. It was so rare and amazing that we would not sell it either. We decided that we would all own it and rotate it from inheritor to inheritor each year. I just got off the phone with

my mom and we think she got it first but she doesn't know where she put it. I was like "Get it put in your safety deposit box!" Maybe this is our million-dollar item?

So back to my story, we divided up the marbles four ways. There were so many that I ended up with about 200. I decided to keep my favorites and sell the rest to help finance my big move. Sometimes I get more for items when I break them up into smaller portions and sometimes I do better with a large lot. It is a tough call. I have done the best with china and flatware when I break them up into small auctions—two dinner plates, for example, or four forks. My gut feeling was that these marbles would sell for more if they were left all together.

I put the marbles on eBay in September of 2002 and we got a lot of inquiries about these little guys. They sold for $436.25 and ended up in Pennsylvania, where my really good friend Melanie lives now. Maybe she can go and visit them.

#28 34 Clock Keys

$0.^{00}
Paid
From: Inheritance

RARE 34 Lot Clock Winding Keys-Antique-NICE!

Description:
Great set of 34 antique clock winding keys date to the 1880's or
so. All are between 1-1 ½" long. Some have numbers on them for
example 5, 10, 9. They are silver and brass and are in excellent condition. My Grandmother stockpiled these for years. Don't miss out
on this rare bunch of keys!

Winning Bid:

$78.^{00}

Ended: 9/21/02
History: 14 bids
Starting Bid: $.99
Winner: Bridgeview, IL

Viewed
000052 X

The Story

Guess where we are? We are back in the Snake Pit with my brother Lee. Just kidding. The Snake Pit got divided up just like everything else did. We bought about one thousand boxes, all the same size (12" by 12" by 24"). Our friends all pitched in and helped us until the bitter end packing everything up and randomly marking the boxes with one of our four names. At this point, I was still in my house in Bellingham, trying to get as much as possible sold before moving in three weeks.

In one of the boxes, I found this set of keys that I recognized as coming out of the Snake Pit. The keys still had a hang-tag on them with my grandmother's writing. I remembered her telling me that this type of key is very rare because it was used for winding clocks, and it's hard to find in all the different sizes. I decided to sell all the keys together as a single lot.

At this point in my eBay career, I had a new strategy born from necessity and desperation. I was starting almost all of my auctions at 99 cents to make sure that they would attract bidders, be paid for and get shipped before I moved. It turned out to not be the best strategy, but I used it for a while. The problem with this line of thinking was that a lot of things would just get one bid and sell for the 99 cents. If I had started them at $9.99 and they still only got one bid at least it would have been worth my time. The reason that I say $9.99 is because that is one of the break points for paying fees to list on eBay. It costs 30 cents to list an item with a starting bid from $0 to $9.99, compared to 55 cents for the next tier ($9.99 to $24.99). Now I always start at the upper end of any range instead of the lower end.

Back to the watch keys. I thought that they might bring in $20. I was pleasantly surprised when they sold for $78. My grandma was right again—they were scarce (one of her favorite words). Cool!

(One of my favorite words.)

#29 American 46 Star Flag

$0.⁰⁰ Paid

From: Inheritance

American Flag-U.S.-46 Stars-1908-Handmade-WOW

Description:
Antique American Flag is 44" by 83". It has the name M.N. Hill on it. It is red, white and blue and in good to great condition. There are approximately 15 small moth holes and one repair job. It is early 1900's—I would guess 1908. There are 46 stars and the pattern goes 8-7-8-8-7-8. These are either wool or linen stars. A great piece of Americana!

Winning Bid:

$66.⁰⁰

Ended: 9/21/02
History: 7 bids
Starting Bid: $.99
Winner: Lafayette, LA

Viewed
 000101 X

American 46 Star Flag #29

The Story

My grandmother was very proud to be an American. She collected American flags. She always voted. She supported her government and elected officials whether or not she agreed with them. She respected and stood behind the servicemen who served for our country. She lived through many wars. Her flag was flown proudly on every holiday. She always felt very lucky to be an American!

This was one of many flags we came across. My grandmother had various flag collections. Some were real flags, like this one, but I think her favorite collection was all the little rhinestone flag pins she acquired. She had a bulletin board in her bedroom that she had covered with an antique crazy quilt and she pinned these flags all over it. She probably had a hundred—they were so cute! I think my sister got the bulletin board but we all got one quarter of the flag pins. I just found my little box of them the other day—I won't be selling those!

This cloth flag was older because it only had 46 stars. We did some research and found that it would probably date to 1908. I didn't think it would sell for a lot but we came to find that there is a large following for older flags. It's funny, but when we were getting this ready for auction I was so careful not to let it touch the ground. I was taught respect for the flag.

This was during my 99-cent phase, so that is where we began the auction. We got 7 bids and it ended up selling for $66. My grandmother loved to sing, and she was a yell and song leader in the 1920's for her high school in Cashmere, WA. I can still hear her singing "It's a grand old flag, it's a high flying flag, and forever in peace may it wave."

Yell and Song Leaders

Ruth Long   Cheryl Sussex   Fern McDonald

#30 Architectural Standards Book

$0.00 Paid

From: Inheritance Grandpa's book

Architectural Graphic Standard Book-1936-2nd

Description:

Architectural Graphic Standard Book is 9 ½ by 11 ¾". It has 284 pages. 1936 2nd edition. In very good to excellent condition. This book belonged to our grandfather who was an architect.

Winning Bid: **$302.57**

Ended: 9/21/02
History: 14 bids
Starting Bid: $9.99
Winner: Syracuse, NY

Viewed

 **X**

Architectural Standards Book #30

The Story

I had a huge RV garage which measured 48' by 24' by 24' tall in my Bellingham home. I had three offices built into it when I purchased my home in 1998. We were using these to sell on eBay before I moved. The couple that bought my home stopped by one day and absolutely freaked out. They said, "There is no way you can be out of here in two weeks and have this place clean!" I admit it must have looked extremely overwhelming to them, but not to someone who had grown up in the business. I told them not to worry as I wondered how I was possibly going to get all those boxes packed back up and into a semi-truck.

My mom had also inherited boxes and boxes of things and that same day she came over to try her luck with some of them on eBay. I watched her walk in with the stuff that she had chosen and I thought to myself, "Good luck! Nothing in there is going to sell and she will be so discouraged."

It was a box of old books. I have occasionally had great success with books, but the successes have been few and far between. My mom diligently went to work photographing and cataloging each item. I didn't have the heart to tell her it was all for naught. She put about 10 items up on eBay that day and off she went back to her mortgage banking job. If she would have put a hundred items on that day I would have thought she may have had a chance for success. eBay really is a numbers game and ten items isn't playing hard enough.

Well, guess who was wrong again? The rule really is the exception. She called me from her office later that day to gloat. "Oh my gosh! That architectural standards book of my daddy's is up to $180." I was like, "No way—GET OUT!" It had been priced at $8.50 in the shop for years. It ended up selling for $302.57 to an architectural firm in New York. I love telling this story because it really freaked me out.

My mom was an only child and she was her daddy's little girl. My grandfather died almost 30 years ago and my mom still really misses him. This sale was very special to my mom because, as she told me last week, "I believe it was a gift from my dad."

#31 Longaberger Basket

$0.00
Paid

From: My friend Grace's inheritance

Retired Longaberger Picnic Basket-1994 Lovely

Description:
This is a lovely Longaberger Picnic Basket which measures 14 ½"
across by 10" wide by 7 ½" deep. It is in perfect condition. It has
two handles and a hard plastic liner. It is marked "Longaberger
Baskets Handwoven Dresden, Ohio USA DRM 1994" in ink on
the base. A nice addition to any collection.

Winning Bid:

$50.00

Ended: 9/27/02
History: 19 bids
Starting Bid: $.99
Winner: Westerville, OH

Viewed

000089 X

Longaberger Basket #31

The Story

My stress level was obviously high at this point in my life when it suddenly went higher. I was out at Ludtke Trucking with my Dad and kids arranging for the biggest semi they had when I got a call on my cell phone. It was from a producer at a new national television talk show—*The Rob Nelson Show*. They wanted me in L.A. in five days to film a segment about eBay. YIKES! I couldn't say no, could I?

It was a timing problem because they wanted to film me going through someone's house and helping to sell what we found on eBay. eBay's auctions are either three, five, seven or ten days in length. This was a Monday and they wanted to film Friday night with results. I would need to have the items up for sale by Tuesday—the next day—and do three-day auctions.

We decided to get a local camera crew and go through someone's house in Bellingham. Then I could fly down on Friday for the show. I started calling around. First I called Sally Huff, who is an incredible artist, an incurable collector, and a good friend. Sally has an eclectic house full of antiques. I called her to get a photo for this story and she said "I was just thinking of your Granny and her incredible spirit." Sally is a gem! When we wrote our first book in 1997 she suggested that I put my grandmother's fingerprint in the front for good luck. I still do this!

Next, I called Cari Griffith, a friend from my monthly Bunco game, who had a warehouse full of antiques left over from her restaurant. Finally, I called my friend Grace Dexter, who had just inherited a houseful from her aunt. I called the producer back and gave him the three choices. He chose my friend Grace.

On Tuesday morning, we arrived at her house with a camera crew. I found a bunch of great stuff and quickly put together some descriptions for the three-day auctions that would end before 5 PM on Friday when the show taped.

We found this basket in her kitchen where she was just using it to hold her paperwork. It turned out to be a special Longaberger "Made in USA" basket and it sold for $50! Grace was excited.

When we did our research we found that Longaberger is the premier maker of handmade baskets in the United States. They are a family-run business that has been operating out of Ohio for about 30 years. Their baskets are wonderful and unique. Just like Sally Huff.

#32 Spool Cabinet

$0.⁰⁰ Paid

From: My friend Grace's inheritance

5 Drawer Spool Cabinet-Corticelli-Antique-WOW

Description:
Awesome 5 drawer spool cabinet is marked Corticelli. It is 21 by 18 ¾" and is 17 ¼" tall. It has some stains and scratches. It is in good condition. It is oak and needs some finish feeder or other furniture polish. One drawer needs replacement glass and one corner of the wood is broken. There are a few chips. Dates to the early 1900's. 5-drawer spool cabinets are very rare.

Winning Bid: **$358.⁸⁸**

Ended: 9/27/02
History: 7 bids
Starting Bid: $99.99
Winner: Marshaltown, IA

Viewed
000410 X

Spool Cabinet #32

The Story

The best thing I found in Grace's house was this spool cabinet. It had the manufacturer's name on the side—Corticelli. Spool cabinets were used in millinery and general stores to hold and sell thread in the 1890's to 1900's. This one was a beauty, and Grace didn't want to keep it. We put it on with a starting bid of $99.

We decided it would be shipped Greyhound and the winning bidder would pay the actual charges. Greyhound is a great alternative to UPS for larger items because UPS has size restrictions. Greyhound allows larger items as long as they don't weigh over 100 pounds. It cost about $40 to send this piece to Iowa—not bad. The downside is that the purchaser must pick up the item at the local Greyhound station.

Grace was also asked to come to L.A. to be filmed for the segment. It was so much fun. We flew from Seattle to Los Angeles on Friday, September 27th, and were picked up at LAX by a driver and taken to a hotel in Hollywood. We had about three hours before the show taped, so we grabbed lunch with my brother Lee in the hotel. Lee decided to join us at the studio. We were nervous about the show and what the items we'd chosen would actually sell for. The auctions were going to be ending when we were in the green room at the studio. They were going to tell us on camera what things went for.

We got to the studio and they needed me to do some voice-overs for the piece they shot in Bellingham. Then we went to make-up and hung out back stage. That was fun! We felt like stars. The segment went quickly and Rob was a nice host. I don't remember much about it except that Grace's things sold for over $600 and she was excited! I do remember that they made fun of me for using a lot of interjections in my listings—especially the "WOW" in this one. I have never watched the segment, although people said it turned out well. I am sure it is painful to watch yourself on national television—I've chosen never to do it. I did get a lot of book and video orders after the show. It was definitely good for business.

The spool cabinet brought in $358.88—a lot more than we expected. It was shipped to a publishing business in Iowa. After the show, the three of us went to the Sky Bar at the Mondrian Hotel in L.A. We had dinner and hung out. It was a blast! We flew home the next day—back to reality and packing up my life.

#33 Pickle Jar Lids

$0.⁰⁰ Paid

From: Inheritance

Pickle Jar/Castor Silverplate Lid-Decorative!
Pickle Jar/Castor Silverplate Lid-Antique-FAB

Description:
Neat silverplated pickle jar lid is 3 ½" wide and 2 ¼" tall. It is in very good condition. It is a newer lid—probably 1970's—and it has a decorative top. We also have an antique pickle jar lid up for auction.

Winning Bid:

$55.⁴⁸/₂

Ended: 10/2/02
History: 20 bids for both
Starting Bid: $.99
Winner: Bishop, CA

Viewed

X

The Story

This was one of the last few things I sold before moving. Pickle jars were used in Victorian times (1880's) to hold—guess what? Pickles. Can you believe it? They used to have special dishes and utensils for just about everything. They even had special pickle tongs to get the pickles out of the jars! Pickle jars were also called pickle castors and these pieces done in beautiful antique art glass with silverplated metal frames can bring in the big bucks. We had found shoe-boxes full of these lids in the Snake Pit. All I had to put up for auction were just two lids. I put them up separately and started each auction at 99 cents. One of the lids was newer—a 1970's reproduction—and one was antique.

I have found that a lot of older pieces, like Victorian items, don't sell as well as newer kitschy things. The things that my grandmother's generation grew up with don't have the allure that things the baby boomers grew up with have. Most of my grandmother's generation was gone and the baby boomers were the group with the cash. My brother and I discuss this a lot and we have figured out that people are trying to buy their childhoods.

Everything is cyclical, so do not throw away those Beanie Babies! In another 20 years, the kids who couldn't afford them in the late 1990's will be buying them on eBay. Metal lunch boxes, Eames-era 1950's furniture and Bakelite are super hot right now. I couldn't get $49 for a French Baccarat swirl teinte perfume from the 1890's, but I could get $107 for skateboard magazines from the 1970's. It really doesn't make much sense to me. However, there are certain Victorian antiques that will always fetch a lot of money and pickle jars (see #53), cruets (see #37), and mourning hair pieces (see #74) are just a few of them.

I couldn't believe it when these two lids sold for $55.48 to a man in Bishop, California. It just goes to show you that you can sell just parts. The new lid sold for $30.99 and the old one for $24.49. He probably had two pickle jars that needed lids. A marriage made in cyberspace!

#34 1966 Pontiac Lemans

$0.⁰⁰ Paid

From: Ex-husband's grandmother
A gift

1966 Pontiac Lemans 326 Engine-One Owner-NICE

Description:

1966 Pontiac Lemans with 326 Engine. Beige exterior-gold interior. 163,964 miles. One family owner since purchase. Original stereo and license plate frames. Fully stocked. Factory overspray. Potential for show car with some TLC. Garaged for 32 out of 36 years. Stealth Goat 2 door automatic 8 cylinder. Clear title. Driven daily until 2 years ago. Not running at moment, needs heater core. Some rust, minor dents, mildew. Power steering Brakes Posi Traction. I am selling this car for my ex-husband and know nothing about cars. It does have a lot of mold and mildew—being sold AS IS.

Winning Bid: **$1,875.⁰⁰**

Ended: 10/3/02
History: 18 bids
Starting Bid: $999
Winner: WA State

Viewed
002587 X

1966 Pontiac Lemans #34

The Story

In July of 2000, we found that my grandmother only had two weeks to live. We made a schedule so that a family member could be with her day and night for those last days. She couldn't talk at that point but would blink her eyes tightly shut for yes. I used my time with her to get her opinion on everything. I said, "Do you want me to buy the business and keep the store open?" No response. She wasn't going to tell me how to run my life.

I said "Grandma, I could insist on a feeding tube for you. Or are you ready to die and go be with Grandpa and Maybelle?" She blinked her eyes really tightly shut for this one. I broke down. Her mother was Maybelle and she had died at age 34 when my grandmother was just 15 months old. My grandmother never got over not having her mom. I once compiled a book of letters written by and about Maybelle. She was an angel. I gave this compilation to my family one year for Christmas. Everyone, including my grandmother, sat down after Christmas dinner to read them. Within an hour everyone had silent tears running down their faces.

I told my grandmother how unhappy I was in my marriage and asked her if I should get a divorce. No response. My grandmother never told us what to do and I really admired her for that.

My grandmother passed away two weeks later and soon after that I decided on my own that life was too short to stay in an unhealthy marriage. My ex-husband moved to Maui and left his classic 1966 Pontiac in my driveway. It went through two harsh winters until he returned and tried to sell it. He couldn't get $1,000 for it in our little town. I told him I would sell it on eBay for him so that he would have money to move to California and follow his children.

I put it on eBay with a $999 starting bid and no reserve. Cars are a huge business on eBay. We had only put up four pictures and soon found that we should have put up 20. Potential bidders wanted to see the engine, the trunk, the bumpers—EVERYTHING! Over 2,500 people looked at this auction, and the car finally sold for $1,875. The buyer lived in Washington State and on a very cold, dark, and rainy (no way) evening a flatbed truck came and picked it up. We left for California and the sunshine eight days later.

#35 Sowerby Toothpick Holder

$5.00
Grandma Paid

From: Grandma
A gift

Sowerby
89.50

Sowerby Toothpick Holder-Witch-Spinning Wheel

Description:

Rare! Sowerby toothpick holder has a witch on two sides and a lady with a spinning wheel on the other two. It is 2 1/4" by 3 3/8" tall. It is basket weave pressed glass in light yellow or ivory. A great Halloween item. 1880's or so. Signed with the usual Sowerby signature on the base in the shape of a peacock head. There is a tiny 1/8" chip on the edge that really looks like it was done in the making. This is a fabulous piece!

Winning Bid: **$235.16**

Ended: 11/1/02
History: 14 bids
Starting Bid: $49
Winner: Gorham, ME

Viewed
000188 X

Sowerby Toothpick Holder #35

The Story

The shop building had been sold but would not close until January 2003, so I focused on packing up my house because I had a REAL deadline. I just left the shop the way it was—full of things that needed to be divided up. I figured I would fly back in November or December and finish it up.

On October 11th, 2002, our convoy started out for California. My Dad and I drove with my two kids in my car. My brother had flown up to take back his inheritance and some furniture at the same time since he lives in Playa del Rey. He figured he needed a 12' truck but I had overflow from the semi, so we shared a 26' U-haul. He drove it with my ex-husband and my cat Kerouac riding along. Don't forget the 53' Semi that would meet up with us on Sunday in Palm Desert.

It was quite the excursion. When the semi was delivered on Sunday, we asked the driver what it had weighed—he told us 65,000 pounds. We figured I had another 15,000 in the U-haul because I had taken up two-thirds of it. I had moved with 80,000 pounds of stuff! Too many things for any one person to worry about.

I decided I needed to start selling more of my personal things along with what I got from the store. This darling toothpick holder was given to me by my grandmother, who else? It was really neat because it had a witch on it and I had always admired it and thought it was unique. It had been in the shop at one point and I still have the sticker from it. It says "Sowerby $89.50" in my brother's handwriting.

Sowerby is a really neat type of hand-pressed glass from England. They signed their pieces with a peacock's head from 1876 to 1930. I always thought it looked more like a seal. The company made glass from the 1870's until 1972 and many of the later pieces were not marked. My grandmother had probably purchased this in Europe in 1960. Sowerby doesn't usually sell for a whole lot but this piece was a toothpick holder and there are some crazy toothpick holder collectors. Also, the witches made it rare.

I started it at $49 and couldn't believe it when it sold for $235.16, especially considering that it had a tiny chip on the edge. Nice gift—thanks, Grandma! I was making money and cleaning up my life at the same time.

#36 Amusement Park Maps

$3.⁵⁰

Paid

From: Family trip in 1978

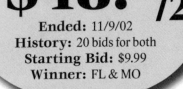

1977 Map Magic Kingdom Walt Disney World-WOW!
1978 Six Flags Map St. Louis-Screamin Eagle!

Description:
1978 Six Flags Map is 23" by 27". It is in excellent condition. My parents bought this for me at Six Flags over Mid-America in St. Louis, Missouri in 1978. It shows the famous Screamin Eagle Roller Coaster.

Winning Bid:

$48.⁵⁵/2

Ended: 11/9/02
History: 20 bids for both
Starting Bid: $9.99
Winner: FL & MO

Viewed

000079 X

Amusement Park Maps #36

The Story

The shock of learning that I owned 80,000 pounds of stuff (I have eight couches) had really set in and I started to go through some boxes that I had kept in storage for years. I love memories and have too many boxes full of them! When we decided to sell the shop and house that had been our hangout for so many years, I just couldn't do it. My therapist, Juna, told me that my memories of my grandmother weren't in the building—they were in my heart. The same was true for all my stuff.

In one box I found papers, ticket stubs, brochures and maps from the round-the-US trip that our family took in 1978. Eastern Airlines (no more) had a great deal that summer—for $278 you could go anywhere they flew. My mom, dad, sister, brother, me and grandma all went. Grandma paid. We went to Illinois, Florida, Missouri, Puerto Rico, the Virgin Islands, Mexico and Trinidad. My grandmother loved to travel and I learned such an important lesson from her: travel as much and as often as you can!

I was about to throw some of the paper items out and decided to do my research on eBay. Can you believe that original Disneyland books of tickets with the most expensive E tickets intact can sell for hundreds of dollars? All I had left in my ticket books were A's and B's. Who would leave Disneyland with an E ticket anyway? For all of you who are too young to remember or not even born yet, Disneyland used to take tickets for each ride and the E tickets were for the best rides.

I found a theme park map from Six Flags over Mid-America and another map and guide from Disneyworld. I put them up for sale separately. Which one do you think sold for the most? I thought it would be the Disney one because of the huge number of Disney collectors, but no—it was the Six Flags map for $27 to someone in Missouri. I think it may have gone for more because of the famous Screamin' Eagle Roller Coaster. The Disney map went for $21.55 to someone in Florida. I was amazed and glad that I hadn't thrown out all my memories before the advent of eBay.

EASTERN

#37 Basketweave Cruet

$0.⁰⁰ Paid

From: Inheritance

Opalescent Art Glass Cruet-Basket weave-OLD!

Description:
Beautiful antique cruet is blue opalescent glass with a basket weave pattern. It is 6 ¼" by 2 ¼" in diameter. It has a tri-corner top with a stopper in it. The stopper is clear and may or may not be original. There is an oval bubble ¾" in the making. It is paneled and quite lovely. I would date it to the 1890's and it comes right off of my grandmother's shelf. There is yellow museum wax on the base that will clean off.

Winning Bid: **$232.⁰⁰**

Ended: 11/9/02
History: 13 bids
Starting Bid: $49.99
Winner: Dalton, GA

Viewed
`000124` X

Basketweave Cruet #37

The Story

My grandmother was a shelf collector. She had hundreds of shelves all over her home that my grandfather had built for her. On each shelf there was a different collection. It was a really neat idea! She collected cruets, cloisonné teapots, paperweights, doll heads, cranberry glass, birds, Vienna bronzes, portrait miniatures on ivory, Steiff, vaseline glass, stretch glass, snow babies, Santa Claus's, tumblers, toothpick holders, Abingdon pottery, banks, St. Clair. . . the list could go on and on, but there isn't enough room in this little book for that.

This piece came right off of the shelf that held her cruet collection. In the mid-1980's, she got very worried about earthquakes, and my paranoid brother didn't help. Every single item in her home was stuck down with yellow museum wax. For a while, almost all of our eBay listings would say "this piece has yellow museum wax on the base which will wash off with good old elbow grease." It was just too messy to clean off so we shipped the items just as we found them.

As long as you let people know ahead of time they will be fine with things like this. It is very important to put very detailed information about condition in your listing or you will get returns. We probably get one return every two months and it is usually because we missed noting some damage.

Cruets of glass and porcelain were made to hold vinegar, oil, and other condiments. They were especially popular during Victorian times (1837-1901) and have been made in a variety of styles since the eighteenth century. I thought this cruet was darling and did think about keeping it. After doing my research and checking other completed auctions, I didn't think it would sell for over $50, so I started the auction at $49.99. Cruets are a very popular collector's item, as I soon found out. This auction was viewed 124 times and I was really surprised when it sold for $182 over my original estimate.

#38 Broken Sewing Machine

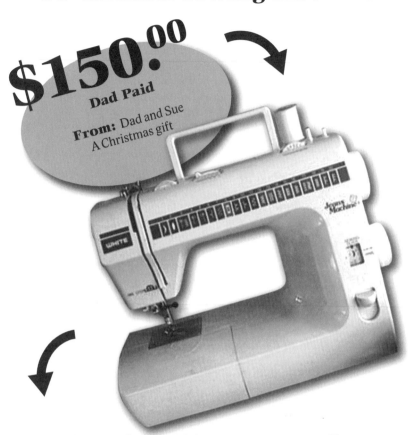

$150.00
Dad Paid

From: Dad and Sue
A Christmas gift

White Sewing Machine-Jeans #1999-Like New!!

Description:

This is the White Jeans Sewing Machine 17" by 12" by 7". It is model 1999 and is in brand new condition because it has not been used very much at all. It is being sold AS IS. The bobbin pops and the needle sticks and breaks. There must be someone out there who can fix this poor thing.

Winning Bid:

$78.00

Ended: 11/12/02
History: 10 bids
Starting Bid: $49.99
Winner: Manhattan Bch, CA

Viewed
 **X**

Broken Sewing Machine #38

The Story

Are you like me? Do you get so busy sometimes that you don't return gifts or things you have purchased within the specified time limits? Do you have bags of things with the original price tags and receipts just waiting to go back to the store? You knew the day after you bought it that it wasn't right but life got in the way. When you finally do go to return it you can't believe that the receipt is dated 65 days ago and they won't take it back? Then eBay is for you!

This sewing machine was a Christmas present from my dad and step-mom Sue in 1997. It was a nice gift. I was always making drapes and stuff and they knew that I could use a good sewing machine. It was an expensive item, but from day one it just didn't work correctly. It would bunch up, the bobbin would pop and it would break needles every 15 minutes. It was so frustrating. Of course I should have returned it then—but NO.

My mom has a Master's degree in home economics from Indiana University. She is an amazing seamstress and cook. She used the machine more than I did because who am I kidding? I don't really sew and I definitely don't cook (the microwave broke last week and I told the kids we wouldn't be eating at home for a while.) I am rebelling against my upbringing. Anyway,

my mom tried and tried to fix this machine every time I got it out for her to use. She finally said, "Return it already."

Fast forward five years. I now live in California with this broken sewing machine. I decided to try it on eBay. I started the auction at $49.99 and waited to see what would happen. I couldn't believe it, but ten bids later it sold for $78, and the buyer even paid the $25 to ship it to Manhattan Beach, CA.

Once again, this just goes to show you that you can sell broken items, and condition does not always matter. It also shows you that eBay can be a great way to get money for unwanted gifts without hurting the gift giver's feelings by asking for a receipt. Just a hint—I have two user IDs on eBay and I sell unwanted gifts under a name no one knows I have!

#39 Americana Quilt

$0.00 Paid
From: Inheritance

Americana Folk/Women's Art Patterned Quilt-Antique!

Description:

This is the classic log cabin quilt in pinks, whites and some blue. It is 74" by 76". It is antique and is in need of work. It is in OK condition. The material is worn and frayed. There is just one type of material. It has eroded in places and there are stains. With some work this will be a neat piece of Americana. This quilt looks better in the photo than it does in real life. No matter how we try we can not take a bad photo.

Winning Bid:

$24.99

Ended: 11/18/02
History: 1 bid
Starting Bid: $24.99
Winner: Williamston, NC

Viewed
`000028` X

Americana Quilt #39

The Story

I got this quilt in one of my boxes from the shop stuff. It was worn and pretty faded. I put it on eBay before my move. I started the auction at $24.99 and the title, which contained a lot of keywords that bidders look for, along with the photo, made this piece look a little too good. Not long after listing it I got an email from a fellow eBayer who helped identify the pattern for us. She said it was the "Sunshine and Shadows" log cabin variation—so I went in and changed the listing to reflect that without double-checking the facts.

Much to my surprise, this piece sold for $93.12. It was the end of September and things were crazy. Somehow we got it shipped out. I soon received an email from the lucky bidder that said:

I bid on and purchased a "Sunshine & Shadows" log cabin quilt. Instead I received a classic log cabin. The package contained an article about your shop and a note from you to Alex. I have the feeling that you shipped my quilt to Alex. Please advise how I should handle getting this back to you and whether you can still send my quilt.

I quickly emailed her back and said:
That is the only quilt we had. We don't know much about quilts and another eBayer told us what the pattern was. Sorry for the mix-up. We will take it back for a refund. Sorry again—Lynn

She emailed me back and said: Lynn, I don't understand. The quilt you sent is nothing like the picture you posted on eBay. Will you refund my shipping both ways? Again, is there a chance you accidentally sent my quilt to Alex? Thanks

It really was the only quilt we had and the whole Alex thing cracked me up. I pulled up the photo and it did make this quilt look great. We had made a mistake and written "Alex" on her paperwork, but it was the same quilt. I did refund her shipping both ways, as well as the original purchase price. Her refund came to $106.12. That hurt!

I did not have time to put the quilt on eBay again before moving, so when I got down to the desert I put it on again. Mari, my college intern, took a bunch of photos of it and we just couldn't get a bad picture of this item. I relisted it but said this quilt does NOT look as good as it does in the photo. I started the bidding at $24.99, and that is all it sold for—but this time it stayed SOLD.

This story is a great example of two things. Never make your item look better in the photo than it really does, and always double-check things that other eBayers tell you about your merchandise.

#40 Navajo Rug

$2.00
Dad Paid

From: Dad
He cleaned out his garage

Genuine Hand Woven Navajo Rug-Vintage-NICE!!!

Description:
Genuine Hand Woven Navaho Rug is vintage 1960's I would guess. It is 41" by 26". It has the original tag which says "Jackson David Co." "Navajo Rugs: A Unique Art Form-Indian Master-piece Guaranteed to have been crafted & woven on a primitive upright loom by a woman of the Navajo Tribe". It is brown, gold, rust, black and gray in color. There is a small hole on the top section but overall in good to very good condition.

Winning Bid:

$67.77
Ended: 11/19/02
History: 12 bids
Starting Bid: $.99
Winner: Boston, MA

Viewed

000055 X

The Story

My dad's wife asked him to clean out the garage so he brought a bunch of stuff over to my house to dump. Thank you very much. That is what I got for living around the corner from him in Bellingham. Anyway, there was some good stuff in one of the boxes and I asked if I could sell it on eBay. No problem

I sold two Cabbage Patch dolls before I moved and got $15 for one and $17 for another. I brought this rug down to California with me and put it on in November—just in time for Christmas. The best months on eBay for me have been September through February. The absolute worst are July and August. I think that everyone is outside in the summer and no one is sitting at their computer waiting to buy. As a buyer, however, you can get some great deals on eBay during the summer.

This piece was really neat because it had a tag on it with its provenance. Provenance is described as either the place of origin or the source and ownership history of a work of art. If you can prove provenance you have a greater chance of getting more money for your item. When we sold all of my grandma's gold coins on eBay, we shipped them off to a professional grader and had them tagged and graded so that we could sell them for more money.

The tag on this piece told me that this was a genuine Navajo rug. With such great provenance, I knew it should sell for a good price. I was still in my 99-cent phase so I started the auction there. It got 12 bids and sold for $67.77—not bad for an item I got in a box of free stuff. Take anything you are offered—free is not necessarily bad! The rug went to the east coast. It is amazing to think—from my garage in Bellingham to my garage in California to being displayed in a lovely home in Boston!

#41 Abraham Lincoln Stereo View

$3.00
Grandma Paid

From: Grandma
A Christmas gift

Lincoln Stereo View-Keystone Photograph-RARE!

Description:

Great antique stereo view of Abraham Lincoln in very good condition. "Keystone View Company Copyright...Made in USA H59 28016." On the back side: "...In this view, taken...only a few months before his assassination, the Great Emancipator stood before the observer with all the startling reality of life. The rough hair and beard, the gentle, far-seeing eyes, the rugged features seamed with lines carved there by four years of heart-breaking toil and anxiety in the service of his country, –all these stood forth in this third-dimension photograph...Keystone...was permitted the privilege of reproducing this likeness of Lincoln."

Winning Bid:

$149.29

Ended: 11/21/02
History: 11 bids
Starting Bid: $9.99
Winner: Boca Raton, FL

Viewed

 **X**

Abraham Lincoln Stereo View #41

The Story

I had a lot of different collections growing up. I collected Canadian silver dollars, Victorian figural napkin rings and bells with people on them—and these collections were all completed before I turned seven! It would be much later in my collecting history that I would actually get to choose what I wanted to collect.

I used to travel to Seattle and Portland with my grandmother to help her set up and sell at antique shows. She did about 15 shows a year. I would miss school and we would always have fun. Usually the shows were pretty slow and we ended up eating a lot of white powdered-sugar donuts with jelly inside and talking. She asked me one day when I was ten, "Who is your favorite president?" I said "Abraham Lincoln" because I really admired what he did to abolish slavery. Right then and there my next collection had begun.

For the next 25 years, all I got for Christmas and birthday gifts was Abraham Lincoln memorabilia. Okay, okay—my grandmother was very generous and that wasn't all I got. I just never had the heart to tell her that I wasn't that interested in Lincoln. Before long, I had postcards, books, bronze plaques, figurines, paperweights and this stereo view. I even had a Lincoln portrait with eyes that followed you everywhere that my grandmother expected me to hang in my bedroom. I hung it behind the door. It freaked me out.

As part of the healing process after my grandmother's death, I decided to sell my Lincoln collection on eBay. Of all the things I had, I thought my Carl Sandburg books (*The War Years* and *The Prairie Years*)—would sell for the most, rather than this stereo view. Stereoscopic views were pictures (often photographs) that appeared three-dimensional when viewed through a stereoscope. They were popular from about 1850 to the 1900's. Until the late 1870's, the corners were square; after that, producers rounded the corners to help prevent damage. This meant that my card had been made post-1870. I knew that stereo view card prices depended mostly on subject matter. I had sold one with a team of horses and workers in a big redwood tree for $95. I was pleasantly surprised when this one sold for close to $150, and the most of any of my Lincoln memorabilia.

As we were cleaning out the last cupboards to close up my grandmother's home, I found an envelope tucked away that said "Lynn Christmas 1978" on the outside in her handwriting. I opened it up with tears in my eyes to find eight Abraham Lincoln postcards. I am not selling those on eBay.

ARTA DIAMOND CORPORATION
9465 Wilshire Blvd., Beverly Hills, Calif. 90212

Lynn
Christmas
1978

Cheryl Leaf Antiques
2828 Northwest Avenue
Bellingham
Washington 98225

#42 Cast Iron Bank

$0.⁰⁰
Paid
From: Inheritance

Cast Iron 2 pc Church Bank-Toy-Antique-Help?

Description:
I think this is a cast iron bank in the shape of a church. It is 3 by 2 ½". It is in very good condition. Dates to the 1890's to 1900's. Antique toy. If anyone knows exactly what it is we would appreciate knowing.

Winning Bid: **$45.⁵⁰**

Ended: 11/27/02
History: 4 bids
Starting Bid: $9.99
Winner: West Warwick, RI

Viewed

000044 X

Cast Iron Bank #42

The Story

This darling little piece was cast iron and I thought it was a bank but I wasn't sure. My grandmother had oak lawyer bookcases all along one wall in her living room with a different collection in each section (remember, she was the original shelf collector). She had a shelf of banks and when we were raising money for the nursing home I had put this one on eBay. I started it at $9.99 and it did not sell. I lowered it to $4.99 and relisted it and again it did not sell. I find that about 60-70% of my items sell the first time out. I relist everything at least once with a lower starting price and try it again. The auction results for any one item can differ radically week to week, month to month and even year to year.

Two years later I decided to try it again. I thought that maybe it had not sold because we didn't really know what it was. I put it on with a "Help?" in the title. I am always grateful when a fellow eBayer helps me out with information. It happens a lot.

One of my grandmother's favorite sayings was "There is no such thing as an expert." She was often called an expert in this or that antique field, and she would say, "There is always more to learn." My love for learning came from growing up around this attitude. I have a Master's in business administration and hope to get a doctorate someday. My grandmother taught classes back in the 1960's and 1970's on antiques and she loved doing it. She would keep examples of everything—antique items and their reproduction counterparts—so that when she hosted a class in her living room she would have real items to show her pupils. The people who were lucky enough to take her classes still talk about them today. She had notebooks filled with one to two pages on every antique category and maker you can imagine. I saved all of these and hope to write a book with them someday. When I started teaching for the Learning Annex, my brother said, "Just like Grandma."

Asking for help in the title lets people know that you want to learn. I received an email from a gentleman that said, "Yes, it is a bank and your dates are correct. To get the money out you have to unscrew the screws." I immediately emailed him a thank you. The third time was a charm. The bank had four bids and the auction was viewed 44 times. This was when I first started to notice that in a lot of auctions it seemed I was getting about $1 for each time it was viewed and this sold for $45.50. That was more like it!

ANTIQUE REPRODUCTIONS will be topic of Mrs. Cheryl Leaf at "Know Your Antiques" lecture Thursday, Feb. 5 sponsored by Beaverton Schools' adult education program. Time is 7:15 p.m. at Highland Park Intermediate School. Lecture, first of series, is open to general public.

#43 Superman Atari Pinball Back

$20.00 Paid

From: Garage sale
Palm Desert, CA

1979 Superman Atari Pinball Machine Back-COOL

Description:

This is a great piece of memorabilia. 1979 Atari Superman Pinball game back is 26" by 26" by 2". It is very heavy. I was told by the man who sold this to me that it will light up if wired correctly. It would make a neat conversation piece. In very good to excellent condition. No scratches and the mirror portion is in excellent shape. Vintage and cool!

Winning Bid: **$137.88**

Ended: 11/30/02
History: 18 bids
Starting Bid: $9.99
Winner: The Colony, TX

Viewed
 X

Superman Atari Pinball Back   #43

The Story

I realized that if I wanted to continue making a good living, I would need to supplement the income from the sale of all the things I inherited by selling items from garage sales and estate sales. I started checking out Palm Desert garage sales in November of 2002. I like going to these sales with a friend—it makes it much more fun and profitable. A lot of times the good sales get so busy that you must have a partner. William, my ex-husband, always had a good eye and we had become friends, so I invited him along one Saturday morning.

We got to a garage sale with a lot of stuff that looked great. I got this really strange feeling, however, that this was a bunch of eBay leftovers. I have a garage full of eBay leftovers—things that you think will sell at online auction that never ever do! First of all, I found this really neat Atari Superman Pinball back. I asked the seller about it. I always try and get whatever provenance that I can. I said "What do you know about this piece? How old is it? Where did you get it?" He said it was from an Atari pinball machine circa 1979, and that it would work and light up when connected correctly. I thought that was great.

When I taught my eBay classes for the Learning Annex, I showed my class a page from eBay magazine that said that Atari was one of the best selling items. "How much?" I asked. "$20." I said "Will you take $10?" My grandmother had always taught me to negotiate, but to do it nicely. Once someone else named the price—you were in the driver's seat. He said "No, I said $20." I asked again differently, "How about $15?" He said "I paid $20 and I want $20." I said "Fine." I was excited to try a Superman piece and even more excited that it was an Atari piece. I remembered my brother in the 1970's playing Atari Pong over and over in his bedroom. People are trying to relive their childhoods and I knew that this stuff was hot!

I dragged it home and Mari Cota, my intern, looked at me and said "What were you thinking?" I knew then and there that I would be packing this huge item for shipping. That was always the problem. Whenever I bought something BIG or sold something BIG in Bellingham or California, my sister or Mari would make me pack it myself. Remind me to never buy anything BIG.

It was fun selling this item. It went for $137.50 and I was excited! We had tons of inquiries and yes, I did pack it up myself, outside, in 100-degree-plus weather. I proved the eBay graveyard guy wrong. One person's trash is someone else's treasure. Yipppeeee!

#44 WA State College Pennant

$0.00
Paid
From: Inheritance

Washington State College Pennant-WSU-1930's!!

Description:

Washington State College Pennant is 14" by 5 ¼". It is felt and in excellent condition. Most of these older pennants have moth holes, but this one is in fantastic condition with no holes. It shows the WSC Cougar. WSC is now known as WSU—Washington State University—in Pullman, WA and part of the Pac 10. Dates to the 1930's or so.

Winning Bid:

$39.89

Ended: 12/4/02
History: 11 bids
Starting Bid: $9.99
Winner: Kennewick, WA

Viewed

 000052 X

WA State College Pennant   #44

The Story

My grandmother grew up in Cashmere, WA. It is a darling town and I was able to visit it for the first time this summer. I happened to be with a bunch of high school girlfriends at a house in Wenatchee for the weekend and Cashmere is the next town. My friend Jo Dallas drove me over to check it out.

I had heard so many stories over the years. My grandma never drank alcohol or smoked in her life—but she loved parties and called herself a "Party Girl." I have pictures of her driving old cars with her girlfriends all over the valley. Her best friend Ruth told me my grandmother was the "ringleader."   The house she grew up in was a bungalow style with a big sleeping porch for the hot summers. I knew about Cashmere State Bank which my great-grandfather, George Sussex, owned. My great-grandfather had loaned money to two gentlemen from Armenia to start their fruit candy company. That company is still in business in Cashmere today and it is the famous Aplets & Cotlets. My grandmother told me that every Christmas they would receive a huge crate of Aplets & Cotlets as a thank you.

She met my grandfather, a teacher at Cashmere High School, when she was a student. She said all the girls were fawning over him because he was so handsome, but she kept her cool and would not let anyone know that she was interested. It worked—she got him!

I had always wanted to take my grandmother back to Cashmere and have her show me around. I didn't get the chance to do it but on that Saturday in August it felt like she was directing us. We found my grandmother's house, the bank, the high school, the candy factory and even the Presbyterian Church that my grandparents had gotten married in. It was really amazing!

After meeting my grandfather at Cashmere High, my grandmother headed off to college at WSC (Washington State College, now Washington State University) in Pullman. My grandfather had graduated from there several years earlier. He was in Sigma Phi Epsilon fraternity and she was in Kappa Kappa Gamma sorority. They got pinned (which signifies a pre-engagement) while she was going to WSC and I have their fraternity and sorority pins in the little leather pouch where they put them on that special day. I won't be selling those!

So when I found this pennant in one of my boxes it brought back a lot of memories. I didn't know if this pennant had belonged to either one of them but I suppose it did. It was in really great condition and I am not a cougar fan so I sold it on eBay for close to $40!

#45 Kartell Magazine Rack

Portariviste Kartell Magazine Rack-Eames-NR!

Description:
Awesome vintage magazine rack is 13 ¾" tall by 8" wide by 16" long. It is signed "Kartell USA" on the base. It is black plastic and in very good condition with no chips or cracks. There are some slight scratches & white scuffs that should clean up. Great 1972 Giotto Stoppino Kartell Portariviste 4-pocket stackable magazine holder with large round handle hole inside. A simple, functional Kartell design that is featured in key literature on 20th century plastics design. Would work well with retro space age designs from the 1950's, 1960's, and 1970's, complementing furnishings & designs from Artemide, Heller, Saarinene and Panton.

Winning Bid: $22.⁵⁰

Ended: 12/11/02
History: 6 bids
Starting Bid: $9.99
Winner: Conestoga, PA

Viewed

000135 X

Kartell Magazine Rack   #45

The Story

I had been teaching how to sell on eBay for the Learning Annex for about two years and it was time to put a new item in my handouts as an example of a listing. eBay was changing so quickly that all my old information needed to be updated. My mom was out visiting for Thanksgiving so we went to some great garage sales. It is always fun to go with my mom. She loves mid-century furniture and accessories and they go very high on eBay. Think 1950's to 1960's space age sleek plastic and Danish teak. My mom buys a lot and has a great eye. Palm Springs is well known for it's mid-century architecture so this area is a good place to pick up these items.

This black magazine rack was at a garage sale marked $2. My mom told me to buy it and I thought it was just tacky office-type plastic. But I usually do what my mother tells me, so I bought it and dragged it home with my car full of other items.

When I got home, I typed "Eames Magazine" on the advance search page in eBay. Oh my gosh! 47 things came up. I scrolled to the second page and lo and behold, there was my rack in white. I opened up the listing and read with much interest that this was actually a signed piece with good lineage. I quickly turned mine over and it also was signed! Me who always turns things over had not even bothered to check because honestly it hadn't occurred to me that plastic of this type would be signed.

The listing that I found talked about the style of this piece and some other furniture designs that it would look good with. I borrowed a little of the listing and added a few other things I found and if you read the description it really does make this piece sound fabulous. These pieces all sold in the $50 range. Score! I put mine up with a $9.99 starting price and no reserve (that is what the NR in the title means). We had two inquiries from Hong Kong wanting to know shipping. It was going to be about $40 airmail, so I think that discouraged some bidding.

It ended up selling for $22.50, a lot less than the ones I found in my research. The ones in my research were all white so that could have been an issue. There was also timing and who was looking that week to consider. I was a little bummed because it was my new class example and I had wanted to show a huge return. My mom pointed out that my rule is to shoot for a sale price ten times what I paid, and this more than satisfied that. My grandmother always said, "You can't go broke making a profit." She was right!

Lynn Dralle

#46 Buechner Open Form Bowl

$20.⁰⁰
Paid
From: Garage sale
Palm Springs, CA

Blown Art Glass Vase Thomas Buechner-Vitrix!!

Description:

Beautiful vase is hand blown glass with a polished pontil. This piece is so lovely it absolutely glows. It is clear with pink, blue and white stripes. It is signed on the base with "Thomas Buechner III copyright 1988." It is 5 ¼" tall, 16 ¼" long and 8 ½" wide. Thomas III was a glass blower in Soho in the 1980's at Vitrix Hot Glass. This is an amazing piece of hand blown art glass in excellent condition!

Winning Bid: **$199.⁰⁰**

Ended: 12/11/02
History: 1 bids
Starting Bid: $199
Winner: Lake Worth, FL

Viewed
000028 X

Buechner Open Form Bowl   #46

The Story

I got this piece the same day my mom and I picked up the Kartell magazine rack. We decided to check out the sales in Palm Springs and one of them was set up in a man's house. He had beautiful things. I think he was really an antiques dealer because he had a large Limoges vase that he wanted $1,000 for. I saw this vase on the table and he had a sticky note on it with the price marked at $35. I said "That is the most beautiful vase I have ever seen. Do you know anything about it?" He said, "It's not signed." I asked him if he would take any less and he said, "Sure, how about $20?" If you first tell someone that their item is wonderful and then try and get a better deal, it usually works like a charm.

As my mom and I were walking out I turned the vase over and saw in the sunlight that it was in fact signed. I was so excited. I said to my mom, "It IS signed!" And she said, "The man who sold it is old, like me, and he probably couldn't see anything that small either."

I got home and immediately got onto eBay to do my research. Nothing came up for that name. When that happens I usually go to the internet search engines. I typed in "Thomas Buechner" and did find a famous artist, but he was missing the "*III*." The Thomas Buechner I did find was the current director of the Corning Museum of Glass and a former president of Steuben Glass. This was getting interesting.

I emailed the Corning Museum of Glass and asked if they could tell me anything. They emailed back and said that Thomas III was the director's son and that he had blown glass in the Soho Section of New York in the 1980's and had owned Vitrix Hot Glass.

I put the vase on eBay with a large starting price—$199. If it didn't sell for that amount I was going to keep it. I got one email asking about the condition and if there were any scratches. I emailed back with the information that it was perfect. It sold and here is the email I received from the winner:

Hello, I wanted you to know that the piece arrived today. It really is beautiful. I did not tell you this before but a friend of mine, Thomas Kelly, who bought Vitrix 6 or 7 years ago from Thomas Buechner, worked on this piece when it was made. Before I bid, I called Tom at Vitrix and had him look at it on eBay for me. He remembered the piece and suggested I purchase it. I thought it was an interesting story to tell you. Thank you again. Happy Holidays. Ellen

I have been in touch with Ellen since and she still loves the piece and will never sell it. She wanted to let me know that it is not a vase, but rather an open form bowl. She also called Tom at Vitrix to arrange for me to call him if I had any more questions. How sweet!

#47 Fitz & Floyd Tureen

$2.00
Paid

From: Estate sale
Palm Desert, CA

Fitz & Floyd Large Pink Fish Soup Tureen-NICE

Description:
This is a beautiful signed Fitz & Floyd Ironstone Tureen. It is 16" long by 8" wide by 9" high. It is a pink fish. It is in excellent condition. Comes with 3 pieces—lid, base and ladle.

Winning Bid:

$48.10

Ended: 12/13/02
History: 12 bids
Starting Bid: $9.99
Winner: Rodeo, CA

Viewed
 **X**

Fitz & Floyd Tureen #47

The Story

It is 4 AM and I am sitting at my computer writing. What am I doing up at 4 AM in the first place, much less writing at this hour? There must be something wrong with me. You see, I am not a morning person and I get up *after* my children, not before. I realize that this book has sparked my passion. I can't stop thinking about this book or going over it in my head. I love this feeling! I sit down to write and before I know it four hours have passed. Time goes so quickly when you are doing something fun!

My grandmother had this feeling every day of her life. She was up at 5:00 in the morning and worked late into the evening, sometimes until 11:00, stringing beads, pricing postcards, putting gemstones into gold mountings, researching her treasures and answering correspondence. She loved what she did. She always told me, "Love your work or else find work you love." She also believed that you don't choose a job based on the money. You choose a job you are passionate about and the money will follow. I loved the antique store and my grandmother, and now I get to write about both of them because of eBay!

Speaking of which, back to eBay. I got to an estate sale on a Friday morning in December a little late. There was already a pickup truck in the driveway full of great-looking eBay items. I kicked myself but went inside anyway. You can find a bargain at every garage sale and in every store. My grandmother called these "sleepers" and she would spend time trying to "smoke them out." To do that, you need to be patient and really poke around. There wasn't much

left and then I looked up. Whenever we couldn't find something at the shop—which happened at least once a day—I would remind myself to look up. My office had shelving all the way to the ceiling and I had a note posted by my computer that said "look up." A lot of times what I was looking for had been put just above eye level.

On the refrigerator was this huge soup tureen. I asked the gentleman, "How much?" He said "$2 and it's yours." I got the soup tureen home and was very pleased to find that it was signed F & F for Fitz & Floyd. Fitz & Floyd began making ceramics in 1960. They specialize in hand-painted ceramic giftware, dinnerware, and collectibles. They often retire their items, which adds to their collectibility.

I put this soup tureen on eBay and it had a lot of action and 12 bids. It ended up selling for close to $50, and now I always look for Fitz & Floyd at garage sales and thrift stores. Take your time and look up! But do everything for the fun of it!

#48 Carole Little Outfits

$4.00 Paid

From: Garage sale Palm Desert, CA

Carole Little Size 10-Black Wool JumpSuit-WOW
Carole Little Size 12 Black Pants-Floral Top!

Description:

Carole Little pant and floral top are really hooked together and are a pant suit. Size 12. In excellent gently used condition from a smoke free environment. Only worn once on a cruise. The fabric is from Germany and it is 26" from seam to seam at the underarm and 20 1½" shoulder to hem at waist. It is 100% rayon. Lovely!

Carole Little Black Jumpsuit for Saint-Tropez West. It is in excellent gently used condition from a smoke free environment. Only worn once on a cruise. It is 100" pure wool and is 23" from seam to seam at the underarm. It is 42" from the waist to the hem. Beautiful!

Winning Bid:

$57.00/2

Ended: 12/14/02
History: 7 bids for both auctions
Starting Bid: $24.99
Winner: Columbia Heights.
Loon Rapids, MN

Viewed
000080 X

Carole Little Outfits #48

The Story

My mom had been lucky selling her own used Carole Little outfits on eBay. She actually got more for them than she had paid! She bought them on sale at The Bon Marche (now "The Bon-Macy's") for about $50 each. One sold for $85 and one for $62 on eBay and they were used!

My mom was with me the day I picked up these outfits. We were at a garage sale where I bought some glassware—my favorite item to buy. My mom was looking at the clothes (her favorite item to buy) on the rounders in the back. She said "Lynn, come on over—this woman has excellent taste and a lot of nice name-brand clothing." The woman was very sweet and wanted between $2 and $5 for each item of clothing. She told us that all the clothes on the rounders were things she had bought to wear on cruises, and she had only worn each one or two times. I put this in my listing's description.

I bought several Carole Little outfits for $2 each and an Oleg Cassini beaded gown for $5. The Oleg Cassini sold for $24.99 to a woman in Seattle who was going to wear it as the mother of the bride. I wonder how that turned out? Keep in mind with clothing that condition is very important. Name brands and quality sell! Also, make sure that the items are coming from a smoke-free environment.

I started these auctions at $24.99—I was done with my 99-cent phase and I wanted to show quality by starting the auctions with a higher price. The black jumpsuit sold for $31 and the floral pantsuit sold for $26. Interestingly enough, both pieces went to different people in Minnesota.

I don't sell much clothing because it is not my specialty. There are, however, a great many people who specialize in clothing and they make a good living doing it. Clothing is great to sell because it is easy to ship. It doesn't require any special wrapping and it can't break.

A woman in one of my classes was buying boxes of QVC clothing returns on eBay and then breaking them out and selling them individually. She said that they also sell their returns by the pallet but she hadn't gotten to that quantity yet. She was doing well with the boxes and never had to leave her house! Just kidding—but her experience proves that you can buy items by the lot on eBay and break them out to sell individually without ever going anywhere. Now that's not very much fun—or is it?

FLAT RATE ENVELOPE
FLAT RATE POSTAGE REGARDLESS OF WEIGHT
DOMESTIC USE ONLY

PRIORITY MAIL
UNITED STATES POSTAL S

#49 Space Age Television

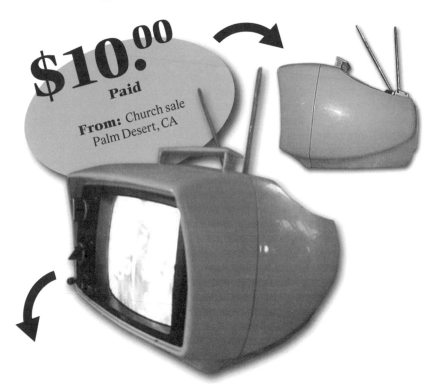

$10.00 Paid

From: Church sale
Palm Desert, CA

Space Age Eames Era Color Television-TV-1970's

Description:

Awesome television is very space age and Eames-era. This white plastic television is a Sears TV '78 and it is 10 ¾" tall by 13 ½" wide by 14" long. It is so cool! It has "March 1978" on it and it still has the original warranty paper tag attached. WOW! It is model no. 564-40190601 and serial no. 583-40112 and "Made in Japan for Sears, Roebuck & Co." It is a color television and it works great! Picture and everything are in excellent condition. The screen is 7" wide by 5 ½" tall.

Winning Bid: $102.50

Ended: 12/17/02
History: 5 bids
Starting Bid: $49
Winner: Tokyo, Japan

Viewed
000114 X

Space Age Television #49

The Story

Let me go on the record by saying that church sales and charity rummage sales are absolutely the best for uncovering hidden treasures. If there is one of these sales listed in the paper I make it a point to be there right at opening. I take my time and I look up and down before leaving. I found this little gem at a church sale on Monterey Avenue in Palm Desert. It was sitting under a table with a sign on it that said $20 "It works." It had already been marked down that morning and the $20 was crossed out and $10 was written.

This television was very space-age and Eames-era cool. My mother describes Eames era as a response to a post-WWII need for a new style of furnishing. Steel, plywood, and plastic were used to meet the demand for more flexible, space saving and affordable objects. Charles Eames (1907-1978), an American industrial designer and architect, is famous for the now classic prize-winning chair that is constructed of molded plywood on metal. His designs span the period from 1945 to 1969, and other pieces from this time frame are referred to as "Eames era."

After hanging out with my mother for the two weeks prior about all I could notice were mod plastic items. I scooped the TV right up, paid for it and put it in my trunk so I could continue looking. I found a lot of other great things that morning.

I got it put on eBay with a starting bid price of $49. We immediately got inquiries from around the world regarding shipping costs. It ended up selling to a man in Japan who paid $50 for surface shipping which took eight weeks. He emailed me after receiving it and said that the power cord was missing. Ooops! My office was a mess and I spent a week looking for it before I decided to clean up my entire office. There it was on the floor. I immediately shipped it off to him express mail and he let us know that the TV worked perfectly and he was immensely happy!

The irony here is that this television was made in Japan for Sears, an American Company, and now this little TV, after spending 25 years touring the U.S., had found its way home to Tokyo.

#50 Remote Controls

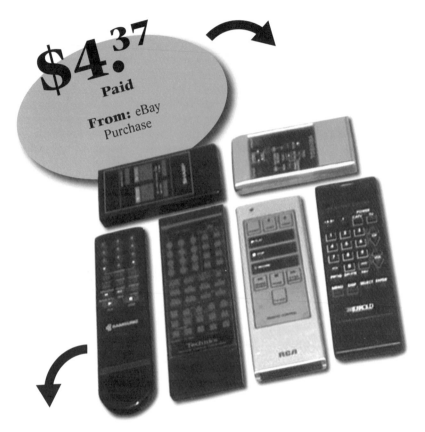

$4.³⁷ Paid

From: eBay Purchase

Lot 6 Remote Controls-Sharp/RCA/Toshiba ETC

Description:

Lot of 6 remote controls for TV/Television. They are in as-found condition. The man who sold them to me told me that they all work. There is a Sharp, Samsung, Technics, RCA, Jerrold and Toshiba. There is also an Emerson that I just found that is not pictured.

Winning Bid:

$10.⁵⁰

Ended: 1/2/03
History: 5 bids
Starting Bid: $4.99
Winner: Seattle, WA

Viewed

 **X**

The Story

After moving away from my entire family, I realized that I would need some help with child care if I were to continue to earn a living. I decided to hire a live-in nanny. I had never had a live-in and I thought I would give it a shot. I made her room very nice and put a Toshiba television in her room. It had been one of my first purchases when I went to work for the May Company. Even though the television worked fine, the remote control was missing and having a working remote turned out to be very important to our nanny.

I didn't know where to begin looking. All of a sudden it dawned on me—eBay. I searched titles and auction descriptions for the keywords "Toshiba," "television," and "remote." Believe it or not, the first time I checked I found one LOT for sale with 8 remotes. The Toshiba one pictured sure looked like the one that had come with my TV. Of course I wouldn't know until I tried it. I emailed the seller and asked if they all worked. "Yes," he said. I bid the starting price of $4.99 and was happy to find that I had won the auction several days later.

The remotes arrived and you won't believe it but the Toshiba remote worked on the nanny's television. Everything was good for a while. I was trying to work out of the home and have the nanny entertain the kids. We found that the kids preferred hanging out in my office to doing anything with the nanny. It wasn't her fault—they just wanted to be close to their Mommy. I had worked outside of the home since they were born and

this was their chance to get my full attention. Since my kids wouldn't spend much time with her, I decided the nanny was an expense I didn't need. But after she moved out, we were left with a great guest room with a television and remote that worked!

I decided to sell the extra remotes on eBay. I tried them on eBay in November and they didn't sell for $9.99. I relisted them at $4.99 and they didn't sell for that much either. I flew home in December to finish packing up the shop and I took my notebook of all my unsold items with me. I did this because eBay occasionally has free listing days and they only announce them a few days ahead of time.

I got lucky—the day after Christmas was a free listing day. I relisted about 150 things that day and the remotes were one of them. I figured that each remote cost me 62 cents— even the one I needed! The rest sold for $10.50 to a man in Seattle. Wow! eBay is not only a great place to buy hard-to-find items, it's also a great place to sell hard-to-find items!

#51 200 Drilled Old Teeth

200 Old Teeth—Drilled, South Pacific? STRANGE

Description:

This is a wonderful collection of about 200 old teeth from some kind of animal. They are about ½" by ¾" in size. They can be used for jewelry and are drilled. They are probably from the South Pacific Islands and brought back from my great uncle Houston's travels. He sailed around the world on the Balea—his sailboat—for years and traded with the natives. These are from his travels.

Winning Bid: $103.50

Ended: 1/24/03
History: 25 bids
Starting Bid: $9.99
Winner: Los Angeles, CA

Viewed
000089 X

200 Drilled Old Teeth   #51

The Story

My grandmother had an older brother named Houston. He was named after their grandmother, Katherine Houston, who was related to Sam Houston—remember the battle of the Alamo? My great uncle Houston and my grandmother were both bigger than life. He used to visit Bellingham every summer. My grandma and I would be diligently pricing things to put in the shop and we would hear a knock at the back kitchen door. I would go and open it and there was Houston. He was full of stories and laughter just like my grandmother. Forget about getting any more work done. They were so much fun to watch!

They grew up together without their mother, Maybelle, who died when they were 1½ and 5. Their father, George Sussex, a banker, did the best he could, and remarried a nice woman. It just wasn't the same for those two little kids without their own mother. My grandmother would often say "Blood is thicker than water." Houston and Cheryl formed a bond that could never be broken.

I got such a kick out of Houston, who was born in 1908, and my grandmother, who was born in 1912, that when my son was born I wanted to honor my grandmother with the name we chose. My son's original due date was July 18th, my great uncle Houston's birthday. What could I do? We named our son Houston. My son is now seven and he and his name are really strong.

For three years, my great uncle Houston traveled the world in his sailboat "The Balea" (Portuguese for "whale"). He mostly explored the South Pacific and would trade with the natives. He would come back with tons of awesome things to sell to my grandmother. They were two of the toughest negotiators I have ever seen. Remember, they both learned their business sense from the same man, their father George.

I found these teeth in the Snake Pit and they were eventually divided up four ways. I put them on eBay and could not believe it when they sold for over $100. My grandmother loved it when we thought she was smart. Boy was she smart. The jar still had her secret code for what she paid on it. I am the only one in the family who can decipher the code and everyone is always calling me for help. I could tell that she had bought them from "H" (Houston) in 1978 and that she had paid $2. She would have been so proud of herself and laughed with delight. She had the most wonderful, contagious laugh, just like her brother!

#52 Brass African Trade Beads

OLD African Brass 200+ Trade Beads—Handmade!

Description:

Antique brass trade beads. There are 200-plus loose medium beads. All are unique, heavy, and hand made. They measure 1/4" to 3/8". Very neat. Date to the 1880's or so—used for trade with Africa.

Winning Bid:

$124.³⁸

Ended: 1/31/03
History: 25 bids
Starting Bid: $9.99
Winner: Zumikon, Switzerland

Viewed
000099 X

Brass African Trade Beads #52

The Story

Over Christmas vacation of 2002 in Bellingham, we divided up the rest of the beads, jewelry and whatever else was good. My brother and I both shipped one more pallet each to California. In one of my boxes I found thousands of these loose brass beads.

My grandmother loved jewelry, especially beads. Big, small, round, square, old, new, metal or glass—it just didn't matter. She was an equal-opportunity bead lover. After my grandmother died, I was in the shop one day and I overheard our good friend and fellow bead lover, Sally Huff, telling another customer why my grandma loved beads and why she had so many.

I said "Whoa—wait a minute! I have never heard this story, and believe me, I have heard all 10,000 of them." My grandma used to tell us her stories over and over again. Sometimes we would hear the same ones twice on the same day! She knew that she repeated them; her defense was that repetition proved that she wasn't lying. "I tell my stories so many times," she would say, "that I couldn't remember the details correctly unless they were true."

I found that the reason my grandmother loved beads and had so many had all started when she was ten years old. She used to go and spend time with her dad at his bank. The Native American chiefs would come in to do business and have strings of beautiful beads around their necks.

She said the strings of beads were piled so high that the chiefs could barely move their necks. She thought the beads were amazing and vowed that someday she would have that many beads.

She achieved her goal and them some. The Snake Pit and every other closet in the house and shop were packed with beads. In addition to Native American beads, my grandma had a lot of African trade beads, which were mostly made in non-African countries from the 1700's to 1900's to be used for trading in Africa.

These neat brass beads had been in the shop at 50 cents each and didn't sell very well. On eBay, I got $124.38 for 200 of them (about 25% more than my grandmother had wanted), and they went to Switzerland, of all places. My grandmother got to buy and sometimes even sell the things she loved. She had the best job in the world!

#53 Cranberry Pickle Castor

$20.00 Grandma Paid
From: Inheritance

Cranberry Pickle Jar/Castor-Enamel—Victorian!

Description:

Beautiful cranberry enameled pickle jar or castor is 10 ¼" tall and 3 ¼" wide. It has a bird finial. Silverplated frame is in good condition but may need re-silvering. The gold on the enamel is slightly worn. 1880's. There is a bird head on the tongs. The frame is marked with 651. Moser (heavily enameled) type florals and very Victorian with dogwood design. There is yellow museum wax on the base which will come off. In very good to excellent condition. A lovely piece from my grandmother's collection.

Winning Bid: **$300.00**

Ended: 2/6/03
History: 12 bids
Starting Bid: $50, $300 reserve
Winner: Winter Haven, FL

Viewed
`000325` **X**

Cranberry Pickle Castor #53

The Story

One of my grandmother's first customers was a woman named Martha Collins. My grandmother would tell the story about how she could still see Martha coming up the front walk of her home on Victor Street when she was selling out of her basement (circa 1948). Martha lived on the south hill in Bellingham and had lost her husband many years earlier. Martha had a lot of Standard Oil Company stock and never had to worry about money. They became best friends.

Martha never had children and was a part of our family. She was just as funny and entertaining as my grandmother and I can remember these two just cracking each other up. They shared a passion for antiques. Martha used to accompany my grandmother to antique shows to help her. Martha always paid her own way, even when she was help-

ing my grandmother for free. It amazed me. Cheryl Leaf had that affect on people. My grandma called Martha her "little pet," which was a Victorian term of endearment. I got in a fight with my friend Peter once, and when we made up I said "We have to be friends. You are my little pet." He said, "Have you lost your mind?"

My grandmother started going to Europe in 1960 to bring back containers of antiques. She was well ahead of the curve. Martha used to go with her and they would hunt for cranberry glass. Cranberry glass was so named because the color resembled that of cranberry juice. It was made both here and abroad and was very popular from the Civil War on.

To say that Cheryl Leaf loved cranberry glass would be an understatement. I think it was her favorite collection. Her entire kitchen window was filled with shelves full of it. She had two pickle castors and was always looking for a third one so she could divide them among her three grandchildren. Since our mom was an only child, we had our grandmother all to ourselves—no cousins to share her with! We called her our Private Grandmother. This was in direct opposition to our Dad, who was one of 13 children!

Cranberry glass wasn't my cup of tea, so I decided to sell this piece. I put it on eBay with a $300 reserve, because for less than that I would have kept it. It ended up selling to a really neat antiques dealer who buys a lot of things from us, so I was happy!

#54 Ikea Work Station

$199.00
Paid
From: Ikea Canada

Ikea Pine Timmerman Computer Work Station—WOW

Description:

Ikea Pine Computer Cabinet is 19 ½" deep, 43" wide and about 64" tall. It is a work station or desk in which the doors can be shut to hide clutter. It is in excellent condition except for a few pen marks. It does have holes already made by Ikea in the back side for your power cords etc. It is the Timmerman pattern from the Ikea line. It has a drawer, a hanging file drawer, a cork board, a white board and a pull out drawer for a keyboard. We will not ship this item. It must be picked up.

Winning Bid:

$227.50

Ended: 2/12/03
History: 13 bids
Starting Bid: $99
Winner: Riverside, CA

Viewed
000289 X

Ikea Work Station #54

The Story

I had tried to sell large pieces of furniture on eBay in Bellingham without much success. Bellingham is not a huge market and people would not make the drive from Seattle to pick items up. It's funny, because Seattle is only 88 miles—a little over an hour away.

I put a beautiful claw foot curved glass china cabinet with gargoyles on eBay. When I did my research I found one just like it that had sold in Dallas, Texas for $2,200. I put ours on with a reserve of $2,000. We had inquiries from all over the country wanting to know shipping rates. We checked with some shipping companies—most notably cratersandfreighters.com—and found that shipping would be about $700. Our china cabinet never went up higher than $1,500. When you add in the shipping charges we were right at the Dallas market price. We decided to sell it in the shop and we got close to $1,900.

I was pleasantly surprised to find that in California it was easier to sell furniture. Now that I am two hours (on a good day) from Los Angeles, more people are willing to make the drive to pick up items. I think people are used to driving a lot in California and it is no big deal to them. I had used this cabinet for four years and paid $199 for it originally at Ikea in Canada. I didn't need it anymore so I called my good friend Melanie Souve who works in the corporate offices of Ikea and said "What is the name for this piece?" She had to ask around but came back with Timmerman. I don't know if having the style name helped to sell it or not, but it is always better to have brand and style names in your title. I was surprised when it sold for more than it cost me new! The people drove out from Riverside one day and picked it up. It was a fun transaction and has encouraged me to try more furniture. Furniture is usually a bigger ticket item and I like those!

#55 Hanging Lamp Frame

$0.00
Paid
From: Inheritance

Hanging Library Lamp Frame-Brass—Antique—NICE

Description:
Nice Banquet, Library, or Parlor Hanging Lamp Frame ONLY is brass. It is 14" where the shade would fit. There is a 4 _" space for a font. It is in excellent condition for its age. Circa 1880's. The chains are 15" and it is 29" tall. The frame is old but I don't know about the 2 side decorations and one lower decoration. It has old chain.

Winning Bid:

$139.00

Ended: 2/17/03
History: 13 bids
Starting Bid: $24.99
Winner: Lakewood, OH

Viewed

000125 X

Hanging Lamp Frame #55

The Story

There was a huge basement under my grandmother's house that was about 1,200 square feet with tall ceilings. This was where she had her lamp department. It was full of antique lamp parts in shoeboxes, on shelves and hanging from the rafters. It was a mess! My grandmother loved antique lighting and knew that it was a good business. She stockpiled.

We would be down there sorting and she would say to me "What are you guys going to do with all this stuff when I am gone? Don't give it away." I said "Of course not, Grandma. You are not leaving me with this mess. You are going to go through it all with me." "Oh, nuts!" she would say and laugh. "I thought I was going to get out of the hard work." She loved sorting and making things out of parts. Who was she kidding?

At the very end of the liquidation, I opened up the basement to the public. I had priced the lamp parts high because I knew that authentic antique lamp parts can sell for a lot of money on eBay.

One lady was chatting with me during the sale, and she asked "What are you going to do with all the stuff that is left?" I had heard that question about 10,000 times before the shop finally closed. I said, "We are going to divide it up four ways. I have been in charge of it for the past 9½ years and it's time to pass the flame. One fourth will be a lot more manageable. My grandmother said to never give it away." The woman said, "It's obvious you didn't price it to do that."

In Victorian times (about 1880's) those who could afford it had fancy hanging lamps with decorative glass prisms in their main rooms. They used them in the living room, parlor or library. See #78 to view a completed lamp. This frame from an antique library lamp was in one of my boxes. Just the frame—no font (to hold the kerosene oil) and no shade (to diffuse the light). It sold for $139! I am glad that I honored my grandmother's wishes and I didn't sell it all for pennies on the dollar!

Love to Lynn, The best manager a Grandma ever had! Love Grandma

#56 Pewter Porringer

$5.00
Shop Paid
From: Inheritance

Pewter Porringer-Crown Handled—18th C.—Scarce

Description:

Pewter Porringer has a crown handle. Porringers were used to feed children. It is 5 ½ by 8" wide at the handle and 1 ¾" tall. One mend in the base. Minor dents. This piece dates to the 18th century or so and is scarce because during the American Revolution many pewter pieces were melted to make bullets. This piece is very primitive and is typical of what was coming out of Rhode Island in the late 1700's. It shows its age and is a wonderful piece of early American craftsmanship.

Winning Bid: **$305.00**

Ended: 3/3/03
History: 18 bids
Starting Bid: $49
Winner: Downington, PA

Viewed
 **X**

Pewter Porringer   #56

The Story

My daughter, Indiana, loves to help me unpack all the boxes from the shop. It is her favorite job. She is such a good helper at age four—just like I used to be when I was her age. One day she found this pewter piece in one of my boxes. I said, "Indy, that is a really great piece if I could just remember what it is called." We had tried it on eBay when we were in Bellingham. We couldn't remember the proper term for it and we put it on saying pewter dish for $24.99. It didn't sell for that and I am so glad it didn't!

My kids both love to help and have even started to let me sell some of their old things on eBay to raise money to buy the new toys they want. As they get older and are able to put things on eBay themselves, it will be a great way for them to earn money for college. If one of their favorite toys happens to get left in my office they freak out. "Mommy, don't sell my Barbie on eBay!" They know I won't but they think it is so funny.

When Indiana pulled that dish out of the box it finally dawned on me—a porringer! Porringers were low metal bowls with a flat, usually pierced, handle from which children ate or were fed. Pewter is a metal made of mostly tin, copper, bismuth or antimony. There was a lot of really good American pewter made from the 1700's to 1840's, when it was used as tableware. It was eventually replaced with glassware and china. During the American Revolution, many pewter pieces were melted into bullets, so pre-1776 pewter is extremely rare.

My mom was in town visiting and she did a great job researching this piece for me. Her description really helped to sell it. Remember, knowing exactly what you have is what helps you get top dollar. With the right name and history this piece went for $305!

#57 Malaysian Mug

Antique Malaysia Coat of Arms Mug—Horn Handle!

Description:
Neat antique metal mug has a horn handle. It is 4" tall and 6" across with the handle. It is marked "12606." It has coats of arms around it and I would date it to the 1890's or so. The medallions each represent an island or state of Malaysia: Sabah, Sarawak, Penang, Pahang, Singapore, Flangor, Sembialan, Perak. There are palm trees and tusks and the coat of arms of the royal family. It appears to be from the Ottoman Empire. It was brought back from a trip around the world by my grandmother's brother Houston. In very good to excellent condition.

Winning Bid: $66.00

Ended: 3/11/03
History: 8 bids
Starting Bid: $24.99
Winner: Covington, GA

Viewed
000084 X

Malaysian Mug #57

The Story

If you don't know what your item is, pay for an expert's opinion and get an appraisal. Some of the top auction houses will look at your items and give you an estimation. They do this because they are hoping to get your piece for their live auctions. Sotheby's, Christie's and Butterfield's all have web pages with instructions on how to do this. If you do have a very expensive piece and you are not an expert, then using a big auction house is a great way to go. Another way to garner information is to ask your friends.

I have two great guy friends from college, D.K. and Hank. D.K. lives in Palm Desert and he stopped by my house one night for a glass of wine. We call him D.K. because on our college semester in Spain, his hair, when he had it, used to stand straight up like Don King's does. For the past 20 years he has been called D.K., short for Don King. His real name is John Lienhard and his family has always treated me like gold. My brother and I and my kids even spent Christmas Eve dinner with them last year. So D.K. was in my office and I was showing him some of the things that I was putting on eBay.

I happened to show him a metal mug with a horn handle and a bunch of medallions around it with strange words. I told him that we had tried

to sell it in Bellingham and couldn't get $4.99 for it. D.K. is a high school teacher and very brilliant. He says, "Lynn, those are the islands or states of Malaysia. It is probably from the Ottoman Empire." Really! That's all it took. Now I had a great title and realized that it had probably come by way of Houston's boat, the Balea, which made it even more interesting.

This time the mug sold for $66 and got eight bids. I called D.K. to tell him the results, and he couldn't believe it! As a side note, be very careful with items having horn or tortoise-shell on them. I put an antique tortoise-shell bracelet that Houston had brought back from his travels on eBay one morning. An hour later my mom says "Lynn, eBay is on the phone for you." I said, "That can't be good." They were calling to tell me that tortoise-shell can not be resold based on the Endangered Species Act of 1973 and they were ending my auction. Pretty serious to warrant a phone call! eBay watches very closely what is listed on their site. Be careful!

#58 Battersea Salt Cellar

$1.00
Shop Paid
From: Inheritance

Russian Enamel Battersea Salt Cellar—Antique!

Description:

Russian enamel or Battersea salt cellar is 1 ¾" in diameter and 7/8" tall. It has a very heavy floral decoration and is just lovely. The colors are brown, white, gold, yellow, orange, blue, purple and green. It has 3 legs and one is squished. We have tried to show this in the photos. It is a very beautiful and rare piece. 1850's or so.

Winning Bid: $536.68

Ended: 3/11/03
History: 9 bids
Starting Bid: $9.99, $99 reserve
Winner: Lawrence, KS

Viewed
 X

Battersea Salt Cellar #58

The Story

I lived in Los Angeles for 13 years and would fly home often to see my grandmother. No matter how late my plane arrived, my mom or dad would drive me right to her house. She would wait up until the middle of the night to say hello and give me a hug. We would pull into the antique store parking lot (which was also her home) and one little light would be on. Never waste power! There she would be working or reading, waiting for me like it was a big deal. She made me feel like I was a big deal. Everyone deserves a grandmother like mine. She pushed me to work hard and be the best I could be and she always believed in me. She made me laugh so hard every day that I was with her and a "Hello, Honey" would do wonders for me today.

It would always be a working vacation for me. A "Busman's Holiday" she called it. "How could a bus driver ever go on a driving vacation and call it a holiday?" We would price and clean things up when I was there. What made her the happiest was when I would clean off her two work tables. I would put away as much as I could and then the rest would go into shoeboxes to be sorted later. I would always mark those boxes things like, "To be sorted," "Never want to sort," and sometimes even "Never, EVER want to sort." Most of those boxes never did get sorted and got divided up just like everything else.

In one of my sorting boxes I found this little enamel salt cellar. I thought it was either Russian Enamel or Battersea. Battersea is a term for enamel on metal, most typically on copper. It was originally made in Battersea, England, but was eventually made in other regions. Boxes were the most common form, and it was produced starting around the 1750's. Did you know that before salt shakers they had to use a master salt and an individual salt cellar? The master salt would be passed around the table and people would take a little bit of salt with a tiny spoon to put in their own salt cellar. Wild!

This piece had a very damaged foot—probably why it got tossed into a sorting box. I still thought that it would bring $99, so I set a hidden reserve with that price. That means that I did not have to sell it if no one bid that high. I happened to be watching this auction when it ended. It was at $103 with 25 seconds left. In the last 2 seconds it went up to $536.68. I was jumping up and down and screaming! Then I called everyone I know. eBay is so much fun!

#59 Pair Vaseline Shades

$10.⁰⁰
Shop Paid
From: Inheritance

Pair Vaseline Lamp/Light Shades—Antique—WOW!!

Description:
Beautiful pair of yellow lamp shades are vaseline glass and glow under a black light. They are 3 ¾" tall and 4" wide at the base. 2 ¼" at the fitter. Pairs are getting harder and harder to find. They have some sharp edges and some chips. Circa the 1920's

Winning Bid:

$214.⁵⁰

Ended: 3/11/03
History: 15 bids
Starting Bid: $49.99
Winner: New York, NY

Viewed
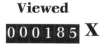 **X**

Pair Vaseline Shades #59

The Story

One summer when I was in high school, I watched the shop while my grandmother went to a NADA (National Association of Dealers in Antiques) Convention in Illinois. She was gone for about two weeks and when she got back she announced, "I did a little buying while I was out there." I asked, "How much is a little?"

The boxes starting arriving about a week later. They were the biggest boxes you can imagine and they were filled with antique light shades. She had bought a collection of 2,000 shades. I can still picture these big white boxes and the butcher paper all over the shop in my mind. It took me all summer to get them unpacked. It was always fun being around my grandma. You never knew what to expect next.

My grandmother loved antique shades. Good antique glass electric and gas shades were getting harder and harder to find and she knew a good deal when she saw one. Gas shades and sets of either type typically sell for the most money.

My grandfather had made several long brass lighting chains for the ceiling that had a shade holder every foot or so. They formed a swag that went down the hallway in my grandma's house and down three rows in the shop. She would hang a different antique shade every foot to sell in the shop, and her favorites in her house. Now we had plenty of shades to sell on the swags! The way

we displayed the shades was unique. Everyone wanted to buy the swags, but they were not for sale. All four of us got one when things were divided up.

Two of the shades she bought that summer were these matching vaseline shades. They were beautiful, and she put them in her bathroom above the sink. When we sold the house, we took them down and I ended up with them. Vaseline glass was invented by a man named Josef Reidel in 1830 in Bohemia. What's unusual about the glass is that it will glow under a black light because it contains trace amounts of uranium. The term "vaseline glass" instead of "uranium glass" is generally used now for any greenish-yellow glass which will glow under an ultra-violet light. We tested the shades under a black light before putting them up for auction, and confirmed that they were genuine.

I thought these shades would go for about $50, but vaseline glass collectors are a very serious bunch. I was pleasantly surprised when they sold for $214.50 and I was reminded of my light shade summer many years ago.

#60 1904 Tapestry

$1.00
Shop Paid
From: Inheritance

1904 St Louis Exposition Tapestry—Square—RARE

Description:
Nice tapestry in earthtones with a lot of green and gold. It is marked 1904 on the base. It is 19" by 19" square. In excellent condition. It is a scene from the St. Louis Exposition.

Winning Bid: **$158.00**

Ended: 3/18/03
History: 22 bids
Starting Bid: $9.99
Winner: Vancouver, WA

Viewed
 **X**

The Story

This tapestry had been kicking around the shop since before we bought a price gun or a computer. When I moved back home in 1993 to run the shop, I tried to get my grandmother to buy a computer to help run the business. It took me six months to convince her. She was a very shrewd businesswoman who only paid cash in her dealings. She had learned business from her father and in a business setting, she was tough.

With her grandchildren, however, she would often say "I am as tough as a marshmallow." When I was really little and stayed with my grandma and grandpa I got to sleep on a cot in their bedroom. For naptime, she always gave me a little pink cup full of miniature marshmallows. I would eat them and stare, fascinated, at a picture of 12 dogs above her door. She gave me that wonderful antique picture and it is in my daughter's room today.

Once I convinced my grandmother to buy the computer, a price gun was easy. It was only $100 and she often said to me, "That was the best $100 we ever spent." It really did speed up our pricing. When I found this tapestry in one of my boxes it wasn't priced

with the ticket gun so I knew that it had been in the store for at least nine years. It was priced at $24.50. We had taken it out of the shop and tried it on eBay and it hadn't sold so back into the shop it had gone.

I had just sold a letter opener with an angel and "1904" on it six days earlier for $45.99. The letter opener also said "St. Louis Exposition" on it and I began to wonder if maybe the tapestry could have been made for the same event. There is a large following for items from this world fair, which celebrated the centennial of the Louisiana Purchase. It was open for about seven months in 1904, and 20 million visitors attended. I quickly got on the internet to do some research. Festival Hall and the Grand Basin were the buildings pictured on my tapestry, which meant it was from the Fair!

I put the tapestry on eBay with this extra information and it sold for $158. This was one of those auctions that still shocks me. We couldn't get $24.50 in the shop for this or $9.99 on eBay, but once we correctly identified it we got over $150! More than enough to buy another price gun!

#61 Danish Eames Catalog

Free

From: Inheritance

Den Permanente ♠ Danish Craftsmen Export Ltd.
Copenhagen · Denmark

Denmark Danish Craftsmen Catalog—Eames Era-67

Description:

Den Permanente & Danish Craftsman Export Ltd. Catalog is from 1967. It has 175 pages and is full of photos. My grandmother picked this up in Europe in 1969. It is 5 7/8" by 8 ¼". In very good to excellent condition. Really great photos of typical Eames-era teak flatware, furniture, lamps etc.

Winning Bid:

$66.⁷⁷

Ended: 3/18/03
History: 10 bids
Starting Bid: $9.99
Winner: Pasadena, CA

Viewed

000085 X

Danish Eames Catalog #61

The Story

In 1969, my grandmother was going back to Europe to buy for the shop. My mom and dad were going along also. We lived in Edmonton, Alberta at that time and my dad was teaching at the University of Alberta. Our neat neighbors, the McColms, were going to watch me and my brother. At the last minute, Nedra decided she couldn't take care of me (age six) and my brother (age three), so my mom and dad had to take us to Europe with them. Score!

It is amazing how much we remember from that trip. My brother's favorite food was the grilled polser hot dog found in Norway and Denmark. He was fascinated with all the trains, double-decker buses and cars. I loved the castles (I AM the Queen of Auctions), antiques, and all the pretty dolls. My parents bought me a doll from each country we visited. I still have my favorite pink one. I was bitten by the travel bug and I was only six!

During that trip and the many others that my grandmother took, she would pick up books, reference guides, brochures, catalogs and anything else of interest. We had boxes and boxes of these paper items when I went to liquidate her personal paperwork. My grandmother had trained me well and I didn't throw any of it away. Instead, I divided it up. I found this catalog from our 1969 Europe trip in one of my boxes and thought I would try this piece of ephemera on eBay.

Ephemera is a huge business both on and off the internet. Ephemera is defined as "printed matter of passing interest," but it holds more than a passing interest to those who collect postcards, stereo views, letters, autographs, baseball cards, Victorian scrap, magazines, newspapers, restaurant menus, brochures, ticket stubs and catalogs. The list could go on, but the point is that there is a very real demand for these items.

I put the Danish catalog on eBay using the Eames era angle. Most of the teak Danish items in this book were very sleek and 1960's retro. It turned out that other people thought it was as interesting as my grandmother had. It sold for $66.77. My grandmother would have been shocked! I am glad I didn't go by my gut instinct and just toss it all.

#62 Poultry Book

$0.00 **Paid**

From: Inheritance

American Standard of Perfection—Poultry-1898!

Description:
The American Standard of Perfection for Poultry book is 4 ¾" by 6 ¾". It is copyright 1898 and 1900. It is in good condition with some cover wear. 255 pages.

Winning Bid:

$80.00

Ended: 3/18/03
History: 14 bids
Starting Bid: $9.99
Winner: Philadelphia, TN

Viewed
000090 X

Poultry Book #62

The Story

Whenever my grandmother and I sat down to price things we always tried to get through a lot of the same items at once. It really saved time. I remember one day we decided to tackle all the old books. There were boxes of books in the attic. There were even more boxes of books in the old brown van, which is where I had dumped a lot of things I didn't want to deal with when I had expanded the store.

We pulled them all together and stacked piles and piles of books in my grandmother's living room. My grandmother looked at it all and said (as she often did), "You know the best part of all this junk?" We would always answer in unison, "It's all paid for!" She was very proud of that fact.

We priced and priced and got a lot of the books into the shop. Many did not sell and I found this one in with my things. It was a very strange book about poultry from the turn of the century and had been priced at $19.50 in pencil inside the front cover by me and my grandmother. I decided to give it a try on eBay

I try to put 100 to 150 new items on eBay each week. Here is my system, which takes me about 30 to 40 hours each week (not including the time it takes to find the items or to answer emails and ship). I take my "I Sell" tracking sheets and number them from 1-150 for the week. I write up 50 things a day on Monday, Wednesday, and Friday, which involves measuring, noting condition and doing research. I also get the photos ready. On Tuesday, Thursday, and Saturday, I put the items I've prepared the previous day on eBay.

I had my sheet for the poultry book in front of me and I went on eBay to do my research. The same title from 1888 had sold for $29.50. This was definitely worth trying but I didn't think it would go as high as that because it was a later edition. Once again, I was wrong. It sold for $80— way more than my grandmother and I had priced it!

#63 Candlewick Dealer Catalog

Free

From: Inheritance

Candlewick Imperial Glass Dealer Catalog-1950

Description:

Candlewick Crystal by Imperial Glass Dealer catalog is 8 ½"
by 11". I am guessing that this catalog dates to 1950 although I
couldn't find a date. Candlewick was made by the Imperial Glass
Corporation Bellaire, Ohio. This was actually used by my grandmother to order for her antiques and gift store which she opened in
1950! The cover is worn and it is missing a red piece of the corner.
15 pages.

Winning Bid:

$77.⁵⁰

Ended: 3/19/03
History: 13 bids
Starting Bid: $9.99
Winner: Evanston, IL

Viewed
000068 **X**

Candlewick Dealer Catalog #63

The Story

In 1950 my grandmother started ordering gift items for her store. Her business has always been called Cheryl Leaf Antiques & Gifts. From day one she knew that the gift business was a good complement to her antiques. It also kept her informed as to which companies were reproducing older glass patterns. Some of the first gift companies she carried were Fenton, Royal Copenhagen, Bing & Grondahl, Imperial, St. Clair and Steiff.

Every year she would get a new catalog and price list from each company, either in the mail or when she went to the Seattle Gift Show. She kept every single one! I tried and tried over the years to throw them out. "No way!" she would say. I was not going to ever succeed in getting these into the "circular file" as she called the wastebasket.

They all ended up in a huge file cabinet in the basement. I was lucky enough to try a few of the Fenton catalogs on eBay while she was still alive. The 1958 sold for $76.99, the 1969 sold for $66 and the 1971 also sold for exactly $76.99. I couldn't believe it and couldn't wait to tell her. When she came to the shop that week I showed her the auction pages and told her, "Grandma, you were right again." She just looked at me so happy with herself. She was "pleased as punch."

This Candlewick catalog from Imperial glass was an interesting one. It was from one of my grandma's first years in business and it sold for $77.50! Then, after the auction ended, a woman who had missed bidding emailed me. She was devastated. 1950 was the year she had gotten married and they had chosen Candlewick as their crystal. She begged me to make a copy of the catalog for her and offered me $50 to do it. I checked for copyright notices and could find none so I did it. A total of $127.50! My grandmother obviously knew what she was doing and would have "laughed all the way to the bank"—another of her favorite sayings, of course.

#64 Tiffany Stamp Box

$25.⁰⁰

Grandma Paid

From: My brother's inheritance

Tiffany Studios Stamp Box-Pine Needle-G Glass

Description:
Signed Tiffany Studios New York Stamp Box is 4 1/8" by 2 ¼" by 1 3/8" tall. This piece came from my grandmother's personal box collection. It is the pine needle pattern in green slag. The patina is gorgeous and the favrille glass is bright and lovely. It is pierced metal overlay. A very rare and wonderful piece which dates to the 1920's or so. It is very Art Deco in feel and is in excellent condition.

Winning Bid: $932.²²

Ended: 3/20/03
History: 15 bids
Starting Bid: $49.99, $650 reserve
Winner: Scottsdale, AZ

Viewed
000542 X

Tiffany Stamp Box #64

The Story

My grandmother loved boxes, so of course she collected them. Stamp, trinket, covered, patch, trick, and the list could go on. Her favorites were the patch boxes, and she kept her collection in a glass-top coffee table so we could look at them easily. Patch boxes were used in Victorian times to hold little black patches. Women would put a little black patch—much like a beauty mark—on their skin next to their best feature. Whether it was their fantastic eyes or a wonderful nose, they would try to draw attention to it. Patch boxes were hinged covered boxes and many were highly decorated with enamel. My grandma had about 150 of them.

This Tiffany stamp box was a favorite of hers—well, anything from Tiffany's was—so it got to reside with the patch boxes. My brother picked this out after my grandmother passed away. He, like my grandmother did, appreciates good quality. Charles Tiffany founded Tiffany & Co. (then Tiffany & Young) in 1837 in New York. His son, Louis Comfort Tiffany (commonly known as "LCT"), founded Tiffany Studios in 1900; it remained open until 1930. Louis Comfort Tiffany enjoyed making household wares like stamp boxes with metal components. He was also famous for his wonderful art glass, lamps, jewelry and enamels. Louis' work exemplified the Art Nouveau style of design. This stamp box was a wonderful example.

My brother decided to sell the box. We talked about it and decided that eBay was the way to go. He did his research and found that stamp boxes with grape patterns were worth about $500. The pine needle pattern seemed to be more scarce. I told him that I thought it was worth $1,000 and he shouldn't sell it if he got less than that. He put it on eBay the first time with a hidden reserve of $1,000 and it didn't reach the reserve. We talked again and he felt that $650 would be a fair reserve. He relisted it with that reserve and almost got the $1,000 when it sold for $932.22.

The buyer wanted to pick it up in person, which is always a little awkward. Picking up items in person was not a problem when we had a store. I guess I do need to open a store in Palm Desert. My brother met the gentleman in a public place. They chose the Hertz lot at Los Angeles International Airport and the handoff was accomplished. This amazing piece of art glass history in the form of a box had a new home.

#65 Stein Lid

$0.⁰⁰ **Paid**

From: Inheritance

German? Stein Lid Only—Harp/Vines 1890's NICE

Description:
This stein lid measures 3 ¼". It is cream and blue in color with a harp and vines. I think it is probably German although it is not marked. I would date it to the 1890's as a guess. It has broken off from the rest of the stein at the handle which you can see in the photos.

Winning Bid: **$39.**⁵⁰

Ended: 3/21/03
History: 8 bids
Starting Bid: $9.99
Winner: Winnipeg, MB

Viewed
000039 X

The Story

Remember those boxes and boxes of stoppers we found in the Snake Pit? Well, there were also boxes and boxes of lids in the old hallway. Glass lids, metal lids, pottery lids, ironstone lids, ceramic lids, and china lids. The old hallway went from the shop to my grandma and grandpa's bedroom and my mom's bedroom. It was really wide, so my grandma had my grandfather build her huge shelves with doors that ran the entire 20-foot length of the hall. There was always a ton of interesting stuff tucked away in there. You would open the doors and this cedar wood smell would come wafting out. I can almost smell it now.

This lid was originally in one of those cupboards and now it was in my office in California. It had a price tag on it from the price gun with season letter "O." I put season letters on every item just like they do in all major stores so I could tell how long something had sat without selling. I changed my season letter every six months. "P" was our very last letter so that made "O" our second to last. At the very most this piece had only been out for one year. It was priced at $9.50 and the last two weeks of the shop we had been at 70% off so this had not even sold for $2.85!

It was interesting, so I thought I would try it on eBay. My grandmother always taught us to be very ethical in business. Never sell something for what it wasn't. Always tell the truth and if you don't know something, "Don't be afraid to say you don't know." I used to love to poke around the shop and read my grandmother's tags. She was so funny. She would write the price and then things like "We don't know either," "What do YOU think it is?" or "Help?" if she didn't know what something was. I didn't know anything about this lid. It wasn't marked so in my title and listing I said I thought it was German and from about 1890. I never claim to know things that I don't and if someone emails me and tells me that I am way off and I think they are right, I immediately change my listing. I don't want to mislead anyone.

No one emailed me about this piece but I was shocked to see that it sold for close to $40. I have put entire steins on eBay and have not gotten more than $10, but we got four times that for a lid. It really is strange what sells and what doesn't.

#66 Doll Umbrella

$3.00
Grandma Paid
From: Inheritance

Antique Red Doll Umbrella/Parasol—1890's CUTE!

Description:
Doll umbrella or parasol is 13 ½" by 11 ½". It is red muslin with lace. It is in excellent condition for its age. The fabric is a little faded and it needs a wash. 1890's or so. It is just darling! It comes from my grandmother's personal doll collection.

Winning Bid:

$67.00
Ended: 3/25/03
History: 12 bids
Starting Bid: $24.99
Winner: Florence, Italy

Viewed
 **X**

Doll Umbrella #66

The Story

My grandmother was a collector from way back. She started collecting when she was eight years old after she found a hand-painted stein that her neighbor had thrown in the trash. She wrote on the base where she found it and the year, 1920. We still have it! She hated to throw things away and always saw the potential in things others wanted to get rid of.

One of the first things she decided to collect as a little girl was dolls. She especially liked antique porcelain doll heads, which were usually white china with black hair and were made in the 1880's. She made the most amazing display with these. The heads sat on the bottom shelf in one of her living room windows and graduated from very small—about ½"—to about 6" tall.

When my grandmother's best friend Martha passed away, she inherited Martha's doll Gretchen. Gretchen was in terrible shape. She was an old bisque doll that had been broken and repaired too many times to count, but my grandmother loved her anyway. She had Gretchen and her other dolls displayed on top of the lawyer's bookcases which were also in her living room. Many were in glass cases but some were out and she had two incredible red doll chairs. One was a high chair and the other was a rocker. The chairs now belong to my daughter. On the very top was this little red umbrella. It was so darling and fragile that I thought I should sell it.

I put it on eBay with a starting price of $24.99. If it didn't sell for that I would have kept it for my daughter to give her when she was older. I called it both an umbrella and a parasol. There is a very large following for all types of dolls and accessories. We got quite a few inquiries on this piece. It ended up selling for $67 to a woman in Florence, Italy. What an exciting place to wind up!

#67 63 Trade Beads

$0.⁰⁰
Paid
From: Inheritance

63 Assorted African Trade Beads—Millefiori—OLD!!

Description:

63 assorted African trade beads. These were made in Italy for trade with Africa. They are antique and date to the 1880's or so. They are approximately 3/8" to 1" in length. They are very colorful and all colors are represented. In excellent condition with a few chips. Millefiori glass and wonderful.

Winning Bid:

$61.⁰⁰

Ended: 4/11/03
History: 11 bids
Starting Bid: $9.99
Winner: Bainbridge Isl., WA

Viewed

000087 X

The Story

My grandmother grew up during the depression. Her father owned the town bank, and after the stock market crash of 1929 the bank was in trouble. Over the next several years, her father, George Sussex, personally paid back each and every depositor out of his own pocket. My grandmother was at Washington State College at this time and she had to drop out her junior year because there was no money left to pay tuition. She never got to finish college.

With money short, the household was always running out of important things like toilet paper. My grandma vowed to never let that happen when she was older. One of her favorite sayings was, "It's good to have on hand." If something was on sale, my grandmother would stock up. Not only did she save money, but she never ran out of anything—ever! After she died, I found cases and cases of paper towels and glass lamp chimneys in the attic. We used the paper towels but divided up eight cases of chimneys. I will probably never run out of glass chimneys!

Since she loved beads so much, she liked to have lots of them on hand. These Millefiori beads were made in Italy in the 1800's for trade with Africa. Millefiori is Italian for "a thousand flowers." Fused bundles of glass rods in different shapes and sizes are cross cut to make these beautiful beads. Many of these beads have been dug up out of the ground in Africa and brought to the United States to sell. I remember many an African trader coming to the shop to sell to my grandmother. She spent thousands and thousands of dollars on her beads. She used to buy beads from an American, Micheal Heide, and friends tell me that she practically put him through medical school singlehandedly.

I found 600 of these African trade beads that she probably bought from him in one of my boxes. I decided to break them out into ten lots. This lot of 63 sold for quite a bit—$61. They seemed to sell better off of the strings and loose. As my grandmother used to say, "I have more beads than Carter has pills." I think she may have been right.

#68 Iron Patio Set

$25.00
Paid

From: Antiques dealer garage sale
Bellingham, WA

Eames Era 4 Piece Iron Patio Set—WONDERFUL!!!

Description:
Really nice iron 4-piece patio set. It has been painted black and is in very good condition but could use a touch up. I would date this set to the 1950's or so. It is very sleek and Eames-era in decoration. It needs cushions. There is a small section of floral decoration on the front of each. Some tiny sections with pitting. This set is really neat because you can mix and match the pieces. There is one arm chair that can serve as a stand-alone piece. There are 2 side chairs that can go together to make a love seat or you can add the fourth piece and make a couch which is 82" long. A great set!

Winning Bid: **$169.50**

Ended: 4/14/03
History: 6 bids
Starting Bid: $99
Winner: Alta Loma, CA

Viewed
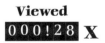 **X**

Iron Patio Set #68

The Story

I bought this patio set in Bellingham several years ago. One of the antique dealers from Old Town was having a garage sale in her basement and my mom and I went. Old Town is a section in Bellingham where there are about ten antique stores all in a row. My Grandmother's store was about two miles from there and the Old Town dealers were always nice enough to refer customers to my grandmother, and she in turn always referred customers back to them.

This black patio set was gray when I saw it and it had cushions. The cushions were cream and I knew the set would look great painted black. I go through stages in my life where I do a lot of painting. I had just survived a two-year white paint stage and was ready for some black. The set was $25 and somehow I managed to get it moved home in the trunk of my little BMW. I think I made two trips. I used to drive all over Bellingham with things sticking out of my trunk. It would embarrass my immediate family members, especially my sister.

This set looked great in black and I used it on the patio of my 1950's Edgemoor home. It fit great with the lines and style of that home. When I tried it on the patio in California it just didn't look right. The cushions had been ruined from all the rain in Washington so I had thrown them away. Buying all new cushions would have cost more than the set itself so I thought I would try to sell the iron pieces on eBay.

I started it at $99 and waited to see what would happen. I thought it photographed great. We had quite a bit of interest and it sold to a really nice couple who drove out from Alta Loma to pick it up. I got $169.50 after I had used it for three years and made an almost sevenfold return on my $25! I bought a real couch and heavy drapes for my new patio with the money.

#69 Pulled Feather Lamp Shades

$100.00
Grandma Paid
From: My brother's inheritance

Set—4 Steuben Blue Pulled Feather Lamp Shade

Description:
Beautiful set of 4 unsigned Art Glass pulled feather shades. They are blue with a gold interior similar to Aurene. Blue is a very rare color in pulled feather. They are 6" tall and 4 ¼" at the widest point. The fitters are standard at 2 ¼". They are typical of Steuben, Quezal, Tiffany or Fostoria. In very good to excellent condition with no chips or cracks. These come right from my grandmother's living room. Very hard to find a matched set of 4 in any maker's pulled feather shade. Date to the 1900's to 1920's.

Winning Bid: $1,400.00

Ended: 4/15/03
History: 11 bids
Starting Bid: $195, $750 reserve
Winner: Fostoria, OH

Viewed
000854 X

Pulled Feather Lamp Shades #69

The Story

My grandmother's living room was beautiful with wooden walls and a fireplace imported from Europe. She loved to take pictures of her three grandchildren in front of the fireplace with her cloisonné plates hanging above. As you know, my grandmother loved lighting and shades. In her living room, she had three brass fixtures lined up in a row. Each held four shades, and only the best would do for Cheryl Leaf! She searched high and low over the years to find three sets of matching shades in pulled feather. Pulled feather was a technique used in the early 1900's by many of the famous glass-makers.

She finally found the three sets in gold, pink and blue. Only one of the sets was signed, and they were Quezal. My brother inherited the unsigned blue set and decided he would sell it on eBay. When he did his research he thought his shades were the most similar to Steuben so that is how he listed them. Steuben began producing the gold aurene, similar to what was used in the interior of these shades, in 1904. We came to find that these shades were in fact Fostoria and quite rare.

The shades sold for $1,400! John and Teresa Weber, who bought them, emailed to tell us that they were made in Fostoria, Ohio. There were 13 different glass companies in Fostoria, Ohio during the years 1887-1920. John told us that these shades were made by one of these companies, the Fostoria Glass Specialty Company, which was in business from 1899 to 1914. Their most colorful period was from 1910-1914 when General Electric owned them and they made Tiffany-type glass. Some of their glass was so well made that it was comparable to other Art Nouveau products—not only of Tiffany, but also of Quezal, Steuben and others!

I asked John how he knew this and he said, "Lynn, we were able to identify the blue pulled feather shades from hundreds of hours of excavating work at the old factory site. It was hands on digging that I did along with my wife Teresa. Fostoria Glass Specialty did not sign their pieces but used a paper label which was usually removed. There is very little printed information for the company, making the discovery of glass shards the primary resource for learning." Fascinating!

John and Teresa bought the shades to donate to The Fostoria Glass Gallery which is a non-profit museum. It is operated by the FOGA (Fostoria, Ohio Glass Association) of which John is Vice-President. My grandmother would be so proud to know that the shades from her little living room in Bellingham are now in a museum!!!

#70 Platinum Cufflinks

$2.⁰⁰ Shop Paid

From: Inheritance

Art Deco Platinum Cufflinks—Antique-HWK—NICE!

Description:
Set of platinum cuff links are 5/8" in diameter. They are beautiful and Art Deco. There is a place for monogramming an initial and it is blank. One of the cuff links is slightly bent. Marked "HWK Co." Platinum. Antique.

Winning Bid: **$145.**⁴⁹

Ended: 4/22/03
History: 26 bids
Starting Bid: $49.99
Winner: San Diego, CA

Viewed
 **X**

Platinum Cufflinks #70

The Story

When my grandfather asked my grandmother to marry him, he presented her with the most perfect one-carat ring set in platinum. The stone was flawless and it was a beauty! My grandmother and I used to talk about how much that must have cost him in 1931 and how he could have possibly afforded it on a teacher's salary during the Depression. She loved the ring but was heartbroken that it wasn't in yellow gold. So, as my grandmother tells the story, "That sweetheart of a teddy bear took that ring back to the jeweler and had it dipped in yellow gold." The jeweler tried to talk him out of it but he was insistent. My grandfather really loved my grandmother.

My grandmother gave me that ring when I graduated from college. You can still see the yellow gold in the crevices. Hers was such a great love story! She never remarried after he passed away in 1976, and she was without him for almost 30 years.

My brother is GIA (Gemological Institute of America) certified, and he would fly home to Bellingham every few months during the last two years of my grandmother's life to help me price the jewelry. Yes, there was a ton of jewelry that had never made it into the shop. We set up our pricing station upstairs in the empty apartment and would sit there for days at a time pricing. He was such a trooper to listen to the horrid Bellingham radio station that played the same 1980's hits over and over.

One day, we started in on all the boxes of cuff links our grandmother had put away. Lee was checking them to see if they were gold or pot metal when he said, "No way. This one is platinum." We both have an appreciation for platinum after hearing the engagement ring story about a thousand times. We priced the cufflinks at $125 and put them in the shop. They didn't even sell for 70% off ($37.50) during the last weeks of the store's closing and they ended up in one of my boxes.

I thought what the heck, I'll put them on eBay and try to get $49.99. Much to my surprise, they sold for almost three times that! I got $145.99, and I also got to remember my grandmother and the platinum ring story when I found them.

Charming Cashmere Bride

SATURDAY, JUNE 4, 1932

Tall Tapers Shed Light On Service

Miss Cheryl Sussex Is Bride at Pretty Ceremony

MRS. ELMER MAYNARD LEAF

#71 Victorian Napkin Ring

$10.00
Grandma Paid

From: Grandma
A gift

RARE Kate Greenaway Silver Napkin Ring/Sled!!

Description:
  Silverplated napkin ring holder is a little boy on a sled. It is a Victorian figural napkin ring and dates to the 1890's or so. It looks like a Kate Greenaway figure. It is in excellent condition and even has hearts on it. 4" by 2 ¾" by 1 ¾". It is marked "Derby Silver Co. Quadruple Plate 370." A great piece!

Winning Bid:

$442.88

Ended: 5/5/03
History: 7 bids
Starting Bid: $25, $199 reserve
Winner: Northridge, CA

Viewed
000125 X

Victorian Napkin Ring #71

The Story

My grandmother had a strong belief and faith in God. She always donated her time and money to help those less fortunate than herself. It was ingrained in us to do the same. I didn't really realize how much this one lesson had sunk in until she had to go into a nursing home.

In 1999, eBay decided to carry my books, *i Buy* and *i Sell,* in their online store. It felt like a great honor. I was working with Glenda Robinson at Ad Gap, the company that ran the store for eBay. We were on the phone one day and I said, "Glenda, I would like to donate a portion of the purchase price of each of my books to charity. Can we put that in the copy?" Glenda said, "Of course we can. I bet that is a lesson you learned from your grandmother." I laughed and said, "You know, you are right." I did donate money to the Toys for Tots Foundation for the three years that they carried my books and it felt great.

I had always wanted to help build a house for a charity like Habitat for Humanity. Early this year, we found out that the Palm Desert Community Presbyterian Church was going on a weekend mission to Tijuana to build a home for a family. Adults and children over five were invited. Indy was only four and a half, but I talked to Pastor Chris and he said we could give it a shot. The three of us went on the trip this May. We were shoveling dirt in the rain and my six-year-old said to me, "Mommy, how much longer are we going to be working?" I said, "Until 9 o'clock tonight." I was just kidding, but he answered with, "No, I want to stay until 10 o'clock and get this finished." What a great attitude, and a great experience for my family!

To raise money to take that weekend off, I decided to sell a napkin ring holder that my grandmother had given me. I knew that these items can sell for a lot, so I put it on with a hidden reserve of $199. Napkin rings became popular in the late 1800's. The most sought-after are the figural silverplated ones made by American companies. That is what I had! I also thought that the child looked like an illustration from a Kate Greenaway book, so I put that in the listing. Kate Greenaway was an artist who was born in the mid-nineteenth century in London and drew young children as her subjects. Her artwork was original and delicate. My napkin ring ended up selling for way over my original estimate—close to $450!

#72 Bohemian Garnets

$0.00
Paid
From: Inheritance

Czech Antique Bohemian Garnet Bracelet—SUPER!
Czech OLD Bohemian Garnet Starburst Brooch!!

Description:

Bohemian Czech garnet bracelet is 2 1/8" by 1 3/4". It is 5/16" deep and has 3 rows of stones. It is missing 25 stones. In as-found condition. 1860's-1880's. This item has been checked by my brother who is GIA-certified (Gemological Institute of America).

My grandmother bought a bunch of Bohemian Czechoslovakian garnets in the 1960's in Europe. All that we put up for auction are authentic and are not new. They date to the 1880's or so. As you probably know, the garnets are real, but were most always set in pot metal.

Winning Bid:

$177.00/2

Ended: 5/6/03
History: 22 bids for both
Starting Bid: $9.99 each
Winner: Munich, Germany

Viewed
000265 X

Bohemian Garnets #72

The Story

My grandmother went to Europe for the first time in 1960 with my mom, dad, grandpa and her best friend Martha. They spent the whole summer there. My grandmother bought and bought (her favorite thing to do). She never spent any money on herself—it was always on merchandise for the store.

Garnet was my grandmother's birthstone. On one European trip, she found out about Bohemian garnets and she was hooked. Garnets come in seven different colors; red was the color of choice in the eighteenth and nineteenth centuries. The most famous garnets at that time were those from an area in the northeastern part of the former Kingdom of Bohemia (the site of modern-day Czechoslovakia). They were smaller stones, but with fabulous color. Bohemian stones were used to make a lot of the jewelry in Europe during the nineteenth century. Genuine Bohemian garnet jewelry features many small stones tightly arranged alongside each other, like the seeds of a pomegranate. The stones were rose cut (as opposed to the brilliant cut of most stones today). They were typically set in pot metal—never in real gold or sterling.

My grandmother stockpiled. She bought all she could get her hands on, not caring about condition. My brother Lee and I priced them all and got them into the shop before it closed. Most were missing stones and were as-is because of their age. My grandmother had planned to repair them and use them to make other pieces of jewelry. She loved to take apart the very ornate necklaces and make smaller, more wearable, drops. I have several of these.

My grandmother and I would discuss Bohemian garnets quite a bit. It was mind-boggling to her that the nineteenth-century artisans who made garnet jewelry spent so much time setting all these tiny tiny stones without putting them in real gold. She would tell me that back in Victorian times the difference in cost between gold and pot metal was just a few pennies.

In my part of the inheritance, I was lucky enough to get one of the glass trays filled with garnet parts. I put a bracelet and a brooch on eBay in May and couldn't believe how high the bidding went. We just show the description for the bracelet, but the brooch was also missing seven stones (although my grandma had it bagged up with seven replacement stones and it was probably on its way to her jeweler). Both pieces sold for $177 and went back to Europe via eBay!!!

#73 Hanging Hearts Vase

$7.⁵⁰ Paid

From: Grandma
A gift

Antique Hanging Heart Vase—Art Glass—Fenton?

Description:
Beautiful art glass vase has hanging hearts and vines. Green with blue outer and a gold aurene inner. It is not signed. It is 3 1/8" at the base and 2 ½" at the top. It is 9 3/8" tall. It is in excellent condition and I would date it to the 1920's. It has a polished pontil. It could be from any number of makers: Steuben, Quezal, Tiffany, Fenton, Imperial, Durand? If anyone knows, please let us know. Thanks!

Winning Bid: $530.⁰⁰

Ended: 5/13/03
History: 18 bids
Starting Bid: $99, $499 reserve
Winner: Burbank, CA

Viewed
000322 X

Hanging Hearts Vase #73

The Story

In 1997, I was working on designing a line of greeting cards. I love antique postcards—guess who and what started me on that one? I was helping my grandmother at a Portland antiques show when I was 13 and she told me to go through all thirty shoeboxes of postcards and take any I wanted. That was the start of my postcard collection!

I thought some of these older postcards could be turned into great greeting cards if they were placed on a border using old-fashioned photo corners. I just didn't know what to use for the border. I called my friend Hank and he suggested postage stamps. Voila! I had an awesome line of cards. I found some wonderful printers in Bellingham, Becky and Larry Raney at Print & Copy, and we found that it was only going to cost $3,000 to go to press. I asked my grandmother for a loan and of course she said yes. She always told me that I could do or be whatever I set my mind to.

We printed the cards and I sent them out to all the major chains. About one week later I got a call from Mike Fitzgerald, the president of Sunrise/Interart in Bloomington,

Indiana. That is where I was born. It was such a coincidence! He said that Barnes & Noble loved the line and wanted to carry it. They would only deal with Sunrise and he offered me a great licensing deal. They flew me out to Bloomington to finalize the terms. My cards were in major stores for about three years. It was so cool!

The designs have since reverted back to me and I decided I was going to re-tool the line and re-print. I needed to raise some money and decided to sell this vase that my grandmother had given me. We had always thought that it was either Fenton or Imperial glass but it was not signed. I knew that the hearts were an important selling feature. I got on eBay and found that they were called hanging hearts. As my research progressed it appeared that it could have been made by any number of makers. I asked for help in the listing but no one ever offered an opinion. I put a high reserve of $499 and it sold for $530! A nice contribution to my greeting card company, Scissors & Glue. I did print this summer and am working on getting major store placement—in my spare time!

#74 Mourning Case

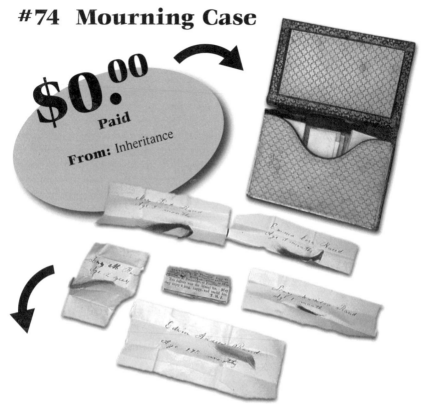

$0.00
Paid

From: Inheritance

Edwardian Hair Mourning Case—Children—Rand

Description:

This is an amazing piece of U.S. history. It is a little leather and papier-mâché case which measures 3 5/8" by 2 1/2" by 1/2" thick. Inside of this Edwardian era case—1850-1870—is a lock of hair from each of one man's children. His name was Thomas Rand, and in addition to the 7 packets with the hair there is his wedding announcement from the newspaper. The most special aspect of this amazing item is how worn it is. The binding of leather is torn from so much wear. Thomas must have carried this in his breast pocket for his entire life to keep his family close by.

Winning Bid:

$127.⁵⁰

Ended: 5/14/03
History: 5 bids
Starting Bid: $99
Winner: Green Bay, WI

Viewed
`000271` X

Mourning Case #74

The Story

This is the story that got me writing this book. The little leather case had been in the Snake Pit for years—who knows where my grandmother had picked it up. I priced it at $55 and put it in the shop for the final days. Even after the price was reduced by 70% (to $16.50), it still didn't sell, and it wound up in one of my boxes.

This piece sat on my desk for several weeks. It fascinated me, and I debated whether or not to sell it. At first I wondered if it were a mourning piece—a way for a father to remember and honor his children who had died. In Edwardian and Victorian times, hair pieces and hair jewelry were very common as remembrances of lost loved ones. I hoped this wasn't one of those.

There were seven packets with hair in the case and a wedding announcement from 1855. The wedding announcement read, "Married on Thursday June 21, 1855 by Rev. TH Johnson of Lattarpe, Mr. Thos H. Rand of Quincy to Miss Catharine S. Swinehart of Pontoosvc. $10 was the liberal fee. May they enjoy a long, happy & useful life. THJ."

The first packet with hair said Edwin Andrew Rand 17 months. The next said Emma Cara three months. There was Lucy Matilda one month. There was another Lucy M at two years. There was Mary Kate three months and finally a packet of hair with no name.

I had a place to start my research, so I spent several hours on the internet one night and found some information about his family. Thomas H. Rand was born in 1830 in Massachusetts. Catharine S. Swinehart was born about 1837 in Ohio. They were married June 21, 1855, in Hancock, Illinois. Lucy Rand was born about 1857 in Hancock County, Illinois. The 1850 census in Hancock, Illinois, reveals that Thomas Rand was age 20 and a tinman. In the 1860 census in the same town, he was a farmer with real estate valued at $9,000 and a personal estate of $5,100. His wife, Catharine, was age 23 and daughters Lucy and Ellen were ages three and two.

In the Hancock census ten years later, Thomas Rand is listed as a hardware merchant with real estate valued at $5,000 and a personal estate of $3,000. Catharine is 33 and the household now includes Lucy, age 13, Emma age 11, Mary, age nine, and Edwin, age seven. There is also Nellie Smith, a 23-year-old domestic servant born in New York. The children had all lived! I had goosebumps!

It sold for $127.50 to a very nice woman in Green Bay, Wisconsin. I was reading my feedback comments one evening and found one that said, "The Best Item I Have Bought on eBay." I clicked on the item number and this is the auction she was referring to. No kidding!

#75 Moorcroft Pitcher

$15.⁰⁰
Grandma Paid

From: Grandma
A gift

OLD Moorcroft Pitcher/Cruet—RARE—Signed Script

Description:
Beautiful piece of Moorcroft pottery is a pitcher or small cruet. 4 1/2" by 2 5/8" tall. 1912 to 1915 or so and it is stamped with a "12" and "W Moorcroft" in a script signature. It is the lovely "Pomegranate" pattern with a green/blue background. Rare piece in excellent condition.

Winning Bid: **$1,092.⁰⁰**

Ended: 5/19/03
History: 19 bids
Starting Bid: $99, $499 reserve
Winner: Monmouthshire, GB

Viewed
000541 X

Moorcroft Pitcher   #75

The Story

My grandmother always loved Moorcroft pottery. It was not easy to find and she only ever had two pieces. One was this small pitcher or cruet that she had bought in England. Sometimes on rainy days we would take a break from pricing and she would show me her collections. She was telling me about this Moorcroft piece on one such day and I told her how beautiful I thought it was. She said, "You like it, it's yours." "Grandma, you give me far too many things." "No, I want you to have it," she said. "Don't say another word." She got one of the little scrap cards that were always around and wrote "Property of Lynn Dralle" and taped it to the base. We usually left the things that she gave us in her home in her cupboards so that she could still enjoy them. But we knew that they were now ours.

When my grandmother started in the antiques business in the 1940's, there weren't a lot of written materials available to help dealers learn about their wares. Antiques reference guides were few and far between. One of the ways my grandmother acquired some of her knowledge was by reading antiques magazines like *Hobbies* and *Antiques Dealer.* One of her favorites in later years was the *Antique Trader.* We bought and sold many things through this great publication. She would cut out any pertinent advertisements or articles and place them inside the items they referred to. This Moorcroft pitcher had one of those little scraps of paper

tucked inside. It was a clipping from the *Antique Trader* in 1990 which listed a Moorcroft vase for sale for $1,010, so we knew the pitcher was a good piece.

Moorcroft was originally founded in 1897 in England as a studio within a larger company, Macintyre Potteries. The designer was 24-year-old William Moorcroft, who soon began to sign or initial each piece of pottery he produced. This did little for the Macintyre company, and in 1912 William Moorcroft went out on his own. He began making his most popular "Pomegranate" ware around 1914. Queen Mary collected his pottery, and in 1928 he was named "Potter to the Queen." He passed away in 1945 and control of the company went to his son, Walter. The company is still in business and their pottery is fabulous.

I decided to sell this piece and found that it had the script signature of the actual William Moorcroft! The other piece my grandmother had was just signed with a stamped signature. I knew this made it a great piece and I put it on with a $499 reserve. It sold for $1,092 and went back to Great Britain. We got more than she had thought it was worth in 1990. She would have been happy!

#76 Electric Guitar

$2.⁰⁰ Paid

From: Thrift store
Palm Desert, CA

1970's Vintage Electric Guitar—Eames Era COOL

Description:

Vintage Electric Guitar is Eames-era Cool. It is from the 1970's and will make a great display piece. It is being sold as-is and the inner bridge needs repair. Approximately 36" by 12". If anyone knows the maker, please let us know.

Winning Bid:

$61.⁰¹

Ended: 6/7/03
History: 15 bids
Starting Bid: $9.99
Winner: Auburn Hills, MI

Viewed

 X

Electric Guitar #76

The Story

I had been making a living selling just the things that I had inherited and a few other personal items. I had not been going out and looking for much. I didn't have to—I had a garage full of stuff! After about ten months of selling off my shop things I looked in the garage and realized that it was getting empty. My grandmother always said, "You can't sell from an empty wagon." She was right. It was time for me to seriously go out and get more items to supplement the things I had left.

I headed over to my favorite thrift store one Saturday morning. The first thing I found was this broken electric guitar for $2. I thought it had a neat shape and would certainly sell for something on eBay. I dragged it home, and my son wanted to help me get it ready to put on the internet. He was just learning to write and he asked me for his own *i Sell* book. He wrote his name on it. Then he got a little yellow sticky note, wrote "Houston doin eBay" on it, and posted it on my computer. Too cute!

My kids have grown up in the antiques business and with eBay. I have been registered on eBay for over five years and it is a way of life for all of us. We even have a picture of Houston pretending to list an eBay auction when he was 2½! My daughter likes to help after school also. After I complete the write-up of an item, she carefully carries it over to the photo studio area. Just as my grandmother encouraged us to become as involved as we wanted in her business, I'm trying to make sure that my kids feel involved in mine. My grandmother always trusted us with fragile items and let us help her. She used to brag that it had been a good investment! We hadn't broken anything of value. She really encouraged us to develop a good strong work ethic at a young age.

So Houston helped me get the guitar ready for auction. It didn't hurt that it was a very boy-friendly item. The guitar sold for over $60. Wow!

#77 Venini Vase

Signed Venini TW Vase—Eames 1966—Murano—WOW!

Description:

This beautiful Eames era vase is signed "Venini Italia tw" on the base. The signature of Tapio Wirkkala. It is 8 1_"tall and 5 3/8" wide. It is purple and green hand-blown art glass done in a swirl type/harlequin cross pattern. When you view this vase, it makes the most unusual pattern from every angle. It is in excellent condition. We date this piece to 1966. An amazing piece of Italian art glass. Venini is the most famous glass studio in Italy and maybe even in the world. Since 1921, very great designers have worked in this studio: Vittorio Zecchin, Napoleone Martinuzzi, Tammaso Buzzi, Carlo Scarpa, Paolo Venini, Tapio Wirkkala, etc.

Winning Bid: **$365.00**

Ended: 6/7/03
History: 10 bids
Starting Bid: $199
Winner: Helsinki, Finland

Viewed
000431 X

The Story

After I found the guitar at my favorite thrift store I put it in my car and decided to take one last look around. I was following my own advice. As I was making my final spin I noticed a glass vase up on a shelf. It was priced $4. I took it down and turned it over. It had a polished pontil. A pontil is made when a piece of glass is blown and it gets broken off. If the pontil is polished, it means the glass maker has taken the time to go back and finish the piece. It usually signifies a more expensive piece of glass. There was also an etched signature that I did not recognize. I will always take a chance for $4 so I brought my vase and guitar home.

I was intrigued by this vase. When the light showed through, it made the most wonderful pattern. In the dark thrift store it had looked to be just one color. I immediately got on eBay and went to "Advanced Search." I typed in the word I could read, "Italia," and then the legible letters of the other word ("Venin") followed by an asterisk. Using the asterisk creates what's called a "wild card" search, which brings up all listings containing any word beginning with the character string preceeding the asterisk. I couldn't believe it, but my search turned up one auction. It was for a "Venini Italia Vase." I immediately went back and typed in "Venini" and about 400 auctions came up. I started reading about the company and couldn't believe how famous it was. And I had never heard of it!

I wrote down some history of the Venini company and included it in my auction description. There were also some initials, "TXX," on the base. I included them in the original listing and asked for help identifying them. A nice eBayer emailed me and said, "It's not TXX, but 'TW,' for the Finn Tapio Wirkkala. He made this particular style in 1966." How cool was that! He was one of the artists that I had listed as famous in my description. Score!

I started the vase high at $199 and it got quite a few bids. When I looked at the bidder history I found that all six of the bidders were from Europe. My $4 vase sold for $365 and we shipped it to Helsinki, Finland, the country of Tappio Wirkkala. My grandmother would have loved this story and been so proud of me. I had smoked out a real sleeper!

#78 Brass Crown for Lamp

$0.00 Paid

From: Inheritance

Antique Brass Crown for Hanging Lamp!

Description:

Antique brass crown for a hanging lamp measures about 6" across. This piece dates to the 1890's or so. Authentic antique lamp and lighting parts are getting harder and harder to find. In very good condition with a slight mark on the outside edge. This piece fits over the top of a 14" lamp shade for decoration.

Winning Bid:

$91.00

Ended: 6/25/03
History: 15 bids
Starting Bid: $9.99
Winner: Williamsville, NY

Viewed
`000052` X

Brass Crown for Lamp   #78

The Story

As we were winding up business in the shop in August of 2002, I invited several lamp and lighting dealers to take a look at everything left in the basement. It was full of lamp parts and we hadn't sold very many in the final weeks. I knew that those parts were going to take a specialized buyer. One dealer bought $200 worth and the other dealer said, "I only want it for a ridiculously low price—so cheap that you will be appalled. That is the only way I will take this stuff off of your hands." I said I would call him if we got desperate.

One of my grandmother's very favorite sayings was, "If we don't have it, nobody needs it." One day, my grandma and I were sitting around pricing and I mentioned that it would be great to have a pricing cart like the one I had used in the department store. I had been an executive trainee for the May Company and we had used these great metal rolling carts. She started to say to me, "If we don't have it..." I said, "I know, I know." She said, "Go up into the attic and turn left. Over the old kitchen you will find a wooden rolling tea cart that should work perfectly." Up I went and of course there it was. My grandmother had a mind like a steel trap. She knew exactly what she owned and exactly where it was. She amazed everyone. The tea cart worked great and I still have it.

Her saying was so cute and so true. I knew that there were some rare lamp parts mixed in with the common ones and I wasn't about to give it all away. I decided to divide it up and let my mom, sister, brother and myself make our own decisions.

I got this crown for a Victorian hanging library lamp in one of my boxes. These decorative hanging lamps generally contained a lot of parts, and frequently included a "crown," which was used to cover up the rough top edge of the lamp shade. I put my crown on eBay with a starting price of $9.99. In my wildest dreams I could not have imagined that it would sell for nearly $100. Amazing! I had it and somebody really needed it!

#79 Eames Era Coffee Table

$5.00
Paid

From: Auction
Palm Springs, CA

Eames Era Coffee Table—Danish?—Sleek Lines!

Description:
Nice coffee table is very Eames-era and looks like teak to me. It feels very Danish and I would date it from 1950 to 1965. It is 21" by 60" by 14 ¾". There is an old moving sticker on the base. It has rough edges and the brass needs cleaning. It needs some TLC.

Winning Bid:

$24.99

Ended: 6/28/03
History: 1 bid
Starting Bid: $24.99
Winner: Carlsbad, CA

Viewed
`000069` X

Eames Era Coffee Table #79

The Story

I was checking out all the thrift stores in my area and trying to get a feel for which ones were overpriced. Most were overpriced. I decided to try going to an auction. There is an auction every two weeks in Palm Springs so we decided to stop by. My mom was in town again with her friend Donna King. Donna is my caterer for life. Every party we had in Bellingham, Donna came and saved my life. Remember, I can't cook. She is a godsend.

My brother was out from L.A. for the weekend and we all headed over in Donna's rental convertible. It was only about 110 degrees! The auction was going on when we arrived. They were selling quite a few box lots, which is a great way to go as a buyer. I have done very well on box lots at auctions in Bellingham. I was going to bid on several, but my brother said, "No." He is very conservative and I shouldn't have listened to him because I let some good things go by. This coffee table came up and it looked very Eames-era sleek to me. They only wanted $5 so my brother said, "Go for it." I bought it. My mom bought a purple floor lamp and we decided to call it a day.

We tried to hang the coffee table out of the trunk. Didn't work. We got the floor lamp in the trunk and got it tied shut. But what to do with the table? I said, "Let's put it between Lee and me in the back seat." Somehow we did it. We were really squished and there were fifty-mile-an-hour winds that day. Lee and I were hold-ing on for dear life and Donna drove us back to my house on the freeway. I kept saying, "This better sell for at least $100." It was so funny!

I put it on eBay with a starting bid of $99. I had some inquiries but no bids. Selling furniture has been a big learning experience for me. We did not deal with much furniture in our antiques store. Everything we had we used for display. I am just starting to get a feel for what sells and what doesn't. I had a furniture success this week, but that will be in my next book. I definitely need to buy a truck to pursue these bigger-ticket items. I relisted the coffee table and dropped the price to $24.99. It sold to a guy in Carlsbad and he came and picked it up. By the way, he was NOT driving a convertible.

#80 Red Waring Blender

$5.00 Paid

From: Estate sale Palm Desert, CA

Waring Professional Blender-PB20—Red—Super!

Description:

Nice Waring Professional Blender PB20 in Red. It is in excellent condition. Large access hole in color coordinated lid for adding ingredients. Easy to operate and easy to clean. Powerful 390 watt commercial quality motor. Crushes ice on both low and high speeds. Heavy duty metal vase. 40 oz. glass carafe. 16 ½" tall and 7" wide. MSRP $170.

Winning Bid:

$51.00

Ended: 7/1/03
History: 16 bids
Starting Bid: $9.99
Winner: Douglasville, GA

Viewed
000057 X

Red Waring Blender #80

The Story

I went to an estate sale in Palm Desert one weekend. Nothing had a sales tag—the sellers were just naming prices. I like it much better when everything is marked. An older couple were in the kitchen looking at this blender and saying how nice it was, but they passed it by without asking about it. I said to the brothers who were liquidating their dad's stuff, "How much?" They said, "Five bucks." I said, "I'll take it." The older couple could have kicked themselves, but they should have asked.

I have found that you need to be really quick when there is good stuff and a lot of lookers. I went to a great sale this past Saturday and I immediately grabbed a box and just started putting things in it. (I can always "edit" my boxes later.) I saw four egg coddlers on a table and knew that they sell pretty well. I had three of them already in my box when a lady came up and grabbed the fourth one right out from under me. She looked at me and said, "I was going to get all four of those." I looked right back at her and said, "So was I." She said, "You are fast."

I took my son and daughter back to this same sale on Sunday because we thought things would be marked down. They were. I had Houston carry my box and all of a sudden he started turning everything over. Indiana said, "What are you doing?" He said, "I'm looking for markings just like

in Mommy's videos. We don't buy anything that doesn't have writing on the bottom." I cracked up. As we were getting ready to leave, I said, "Let's take one more look around." Houston said, "Yes, and we must go slowly so that we don't miss anything." I said "Where did you get that from?" He answered, "From your videos." My kids watch them over and over again, and apparently know more than I do!

This blender turned out to be a very popular one and we got some manufacturer's details from the Waring web site to use in our listing. It sold for $51. As my grandmother would say, "The early bird gets the worm." But you have to be quick, too!

#81 Midwinter Dishes

3 Midwinter Stonehenge Wild Oats Porridge Pots

Description:
This pattern is Midwinter Stonehenge Wild Oats made by Wedgwood England. We have quite a few pieces up for auction this week so save on shipping with multiple purchases. This auction is for 3 Porridge Pots which are a very rare shape. Two are in excellent condition and one has a crack. 4 ¾" by 2 ¼".

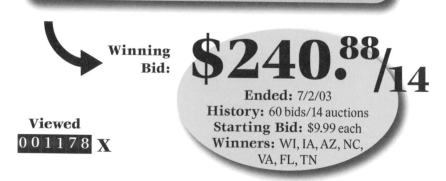

Winning Bid: **$240.⁸⁸/14**

Ended: 7/2/03
History: 60 bids/14 auctions
Starting Bid: $9.99 each
Winners: WI, IA, AZ, NC, VA, FL, TN

Viewed
001178 X

Midwinter Dishes #81

The Story

My grandmother liked to buy by the box, the tableful or the houseful. She would buy entire estates. She bought an estate once with my dad—the estate of Preston Pym. We had Pym stuff around for years. The Pym estate included this one really grotesque yellow doll. I would come home late when I was in high school and find that my brother had left it hanging on a hanger in my closet. "AAAAAHHHHH." He thought he was so funny. We learned a lot of these pranks from our grandmother. She was a relentless jokester. Every year for Christmas, we would "re-gift" a disgusting green doll head she had found and given to one of us as a joke. It made the rounds of our family over the Christmases; when my grandmother got it, she would just laugh and laugh.

I went to a charity sale one Saturday and there were boxes of stuff on the ground under the tables—a great place to look. I found a little square box with four Dansk mugs on the top. There was some brown china in the bottom that typically doesn't sell very well. I asked, "How much?" and they said $5. I decided to risk it and hoped that there would be more Dansk in the box that I couldn't see.

When I got home and unpacked the box, there were only the four pieces of Dansk, along with thirty small pieces of the brown china. I turned a piece over and discovered that it was at least Wedgwood. I got on eBay and went to "Advanced Search" to do my research. I typed in "Midwinter Stonehenge Wild Oats" and a hundred items came up. Typically, there are a good percentage of auctions that end with no bids. What I couldn't believe was that almost all of the Midwinter had sold! This was a very popular pattern.

When I sell china on eBay, I break it out into small lots of between two and four pieces. In this box, I had found one pitcher, seven cereal bowls, five small plates, four cups and saucers, three custard cups, six berry bowls, three porridge pots and one mug. I made 14 auction listings out of these pieces.

The lot that sold for the most was the three porridge pots for $38.99, and it's the description for that auction we've included here. Overall, these pieces added up to $240.88! They were shipped to seven different people in seven states. I couldn't believe it. My grandmother always said, "Leave you own tastes outside the door when you buy." She was right!

#82 Christofle Ice Bucket/Tray

$5.⁰⁰

Paid

From: Garage sale
Palm Desert, CA

Christofle Signed France Silver Tray—Vintage!

Description:

Awesome Christofle France tray is signed on the top side. The tray is very art deco/Eames era. It is 10 ½" by 8". It is in very good condition with some wear and scratches. It should polish up just great because this is from an expensive and wonderful company. Dates to the 1940's to 1950's. We also have a signed Christofle ice bucket up for auction. They may go together.

Winning Bid:

$119.⁸⁹/2

Ended: 7/5/03
History: 14 bids for both
Starting Bid: $9.99 each
Winner: MD & CA

Viewed

000436 X

Christofle Ice Bucket/Tray #82

The Story

I went to an amazing garage sale one day right in my neighborhood. It looked like they had owned a store and these were their leftovers. Nothing was priced so I put everything I wanted on a table and the man named a price. Remember, "Buy by the table." I bought several tablefuls that day and after I got it all home I decided I should go back and take another look.

When I did, I found this silver-plated ice bucket and tray that the seller wanted $5 for. I had passed on it the first time. I asked him if he knew anything about it and he told me that Christofle was a very good brand. I took a chance on it and also bought a few more things.

I got back to my house and started to do my research. Christofle was a good brand and there were over 800 pieces of it listed on eBay. The most expensive was a tea set that had sold for $5,000. Wow!

Christofle was founded in 1830 in Paris by a jeweler named Charles Christofle who had decided to change professions after buying several silver-plating patents. He went on to create the first silverplated holloware factory and eventually became the supplier to Napoleon III. The company is still in business and has always collaborated with great designers. I found that Christofle had even worked with Tapio Wirkkala in the 1950's and 1960's. Wirkalla was the maker of my Venini vase (#77). Goosebumps!

I asked Mari to take the photos for me. I'm sure some of you have noticed that there are some very unprofessional photos out on eBay and other auction sites. They show the seller's living room, kitchen or husband sitting in his easy chair. It doesn't make you want to buy, now does it? We have a photo studio set up in my office. We use a nice curtain for a backdrop. We've learned to be very careful when taking photos of chrome, silverplate or mirrors (it's hard to avoid showing up in the reflection). Getting a good shot of a reflective piece can be tricky!

Mari always takes the best pictures! We put these auctions on separately and, interestingly enough, they did not sell to the same person. The tray went for the most ($66) to a buyer in Germantown, MD, and that is the auction description we show here. The ice bucket went for $53.89 to a bidder in Santa Barbara, CA. It can't hurt to go back to a good garage sale after it has quieted down!

#83 Sitzendorf Girl with Lamb

$3.50
Grandma Paid

From: My brother's inheritance

Sitzendorf Girl w/Lamb Figure 1900s—Excellent

Description:
You are bidding on a 4.5" tall figurine of a girl holding a lamb. It is stamped with the crowned "S" of the Sitzendorf porcelain factory. It was made in the earlier part of the previous century. It is in excellent condition with no chips, cracks or repairs. There is a dark mark on her right arm just in front of her elbow which appears to be in the making. It is a graceful piece and will make a great addition to a Sitzendorf, figural or animal collection.

Winning Bid:

$281.55

Ended: 7/10/03
History: 6 bids
Starting Bid: $24.95
Winner: San Francisco, CA

Viewed
000128 X

Sitzendorf Girl with Lamb   #83

The Story

When I moved back to Bellingham in 1993 to run the store for my grandmother I saw this little figurine in the glass front china cabinet to the right of the front door. It was priced at $350 and the price tag said that it might be Dresden. It was amazing that the figurine stood out against the pink shop walls. When my grandmother bought her building in 1950, the outside was turquoise and pink, with interior walls to match. How mod was that? The shop had pink walls for 43 years. That was all about to change.

The first thing I wanted to do was paint. I said to my grandmother, "Would you mind if I painted the walls white?" She said "What's keeping you? Get to the paint store NOW." As we painted, we classified all the merchandise. We got all the cups and saucers together, all the primitives in one area, all the jewelry in one place, and so on. It took us about six months to move everything and get the shop painted. Everyone pitched in and boy, did the place look great! My grandmother was so proud. We did a whole ad campaign around the remodel.

This little figurine survived the transition and so did all of us. Over the nine years I ran the store, our business increased tenfold. eBay was a big part of that increase. I tried this figurine on eBay using "Dresden" in the title. It did not sell for $50 so I put it back into the shop. My brother wound up with it in one of his boxes. He wanted to identify it correctly before trying to sell it again. He posted pictures of it on a web site, www.porcelainsite.com. Some very nice people emailed him and told him that it was the signature of Sitzendorf. How smart is my brother?

The city of Sitzendorf, Germany, has a porcelain-production history dating back to about 1760. In 1884, the Sitzendorf porcelain company began to produce lace figures in the Dresden style. The company is still in business today.

Once this piece was correctly identified, it sold for $281.55—pretty close to my grandmother's original estimate of $350 (and the Dresden guess wasn't far off either)! Good job!

#84 Planter's Peanut Lid

Planters Peanut Store/Counter Jar Lid—Antique

Description:
Planters Peanut/Peanuts store or counter jar LID only is from the 1940's or so. It needs a cleaning. It is 5 ¾" at the rim and 7 1/8" at the outer edge. There are 2 flake chips underneath. One is 7/8" by 3/8" and one is 5/8" by 3/8". If you have the jar—what a find! These lids are hard to come by!!

Winning Bid:

$42.^{00}

Ended: 7/22/03
History: 15 bids
Starting Bid: $9.99
Winner: Nipomo, CA

Viewed
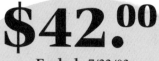
000068 X

Planter's Peanut Lid #84

The Story

One of my grandmother's favorite rooms was the kitchen. Not only was the kitchen window covered with her precious cranberry glass, but she loved to cook and eat. She obviously didn't teach me everything she knew because I certainly can't cook. Whenever we came over, she would ask, "Are you hungry? Let me fix you something to eat." She always had a fully stocked kitchen. Remember, "It's good to have on hand."

While I was away at college and during the eight years after, she would write me frequently and always end her letters with "XOXOXO hugs and kisses." She would often include a $5 bill and tell me it was "To add to your Lincoln collection." She had a great sense of humor. She would also send care packages that contained things like tuna fish and macaroni and cheese right out of her kitchen. She knew I was living on a tight budget and she loved to help. She would always tuck a self-addressed stamped envelope inside those packages to encourage me to write back.

Back to that fully stocked kitchen. On the counters were wonderful big round jars from the old-time grocery stores. They were filled with flour and sugar. One of the smaller ones held crackers that my sister's dog Caesar loved to eat. My sister loves that dog—therefore, so did my grandmother. Caesar came over to visit almost every day and my grandma got a real kick out of feeding him. She would make him sit directly in front of her wheelchair before throwing a cracker in the air for him to catch. "No begging," she would say.

This Planter's lid was from the same type of jar that she had on the counter in her kitchen. Planter's Peanuts was founded in 1906 by two peanut specialists. One of the best known and longer-lived trademarks in American corporate history, Mr. Peanut was the brainchild of a 14-year-old boy who entered a Planter's-sponsored contest in 1916. The boy's winning drawing was a peanut with arms and legs that he had labeled Mr. Peanut. It was later enhanced by Planter's to include the top hat, monocle and cane. Planter's Peanuts items are very collectible. There were over 1,600 completed Planter's auctions listed for the past 30 days when I did my research.

This lid had a couple of chips but it sold for $42 even without the base!

#85 Double Wick Burner

Duplex Antique Double Burner/Knobs/Wicks—NICE

Description:
This is a duplex double burner with two knobs and a place for two wicks. It is antique, dating from about 1890 to 1920. It is bent at the top, otherwise in very good condition. It will hold a 2 ½" chimney, has 1 ½" threads at the base and is 3" tall.

Winning Bid:

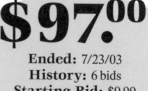

$97.00

Ended: 7/23/03
History: 6 bids
Starting Bid: $9.99
Winner: Stockton, CA

Viewed

000075 X

Double Wick Burner #85

The Story

I celebrated a big birthday this summer and I decided to spend it in Spain. I hadn't been back to Europe since college and it was high time. My kids and I were also going up to spend the summer in Bellingham to escape the heat and see family. I worked it out with my darling dad that I would fly from Palm Springs to Madrid and then Madrid to Seattle. He would fly down in June and drive my kids to Bellingham in my car. I got out of a 1,400-mile road trip. Sweet!

I was able to get 300 auctions ready early to cover the three weeks I wouldn't be able to put things on eBay. eBay has this great feature now where you can schedule the start date up to three weeks out. It costs an extra ten cents but it's worth it. While I was vacationing in Spain, eBay was automatically starting my auctions! It was so neat to be hanging out in Madrid with my mom and sister and have my work already done. We had a blast in Madrid and Valencia. My sister, Kristin, and I were even able to fly home first-class using all the miles I had earned for charging my eBay fees on American Express!

This auction was one of those that started while I was away. The item up for sale was just a duplex burner for a kerosene oil lamp—nothing else. The duplex burner was developed by Joseph Hinks in 1865; it consisted of two flat wicks parallel to each other. It was the most important English design for a burner, and is still being made today. I had scheduled the auction to start on July 16th and I started the bidding at $9.99.

My grandmother always told people who wanted to know what something was worth, "I can't tell you until I have sold it. It's worth what you can get—for you and for me." You can have an appraisal that says an item is worth $10,000, but if you don't have someone willing to pay that, then it's not worth it.

This lamp part sold for $97! I am glad that I didn't sell it to the antiques dealer for what it was worth to him—pennies. It was worth a whole lot more to me! Of course, I didn't know this until after I had sold it.

#86 Purple Tourister Luggage

$10.⁰⁰/4

Paid

From: Charity sale
Issaquah, WA

Vintage Train Case—American Tourister—PURPLE!

Description:

You are not bidding on the entire set—ONLY ONE piece. This is a fantastic Train Case done in a pearlized plum color. It is just lovely. American Tourister size 9" by 8" by 14". This piece is very clean and sweet. A few marks and it could use a cleaning. Pink floral interior with a few stains. Sorry no keys. If you travel with this piece, people will definitely stop you and ask, "Where in the world did you get it?"

Winning Bid:

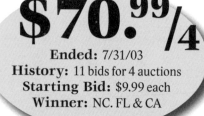

$70.⁹⁹/4

Ended: 7/31/03
History: 11 bids for 4 auctions
Starting Bid: $9.99 each
Winner: NC. FL & CA

Viewed

000124 X

Purple Tourister Luggage #86

The Story

The beauty of selling at online auction is that you can live almost anywhere. We had a great summer up in Bellingham. Doing eBay from Washington State was fun. I got to go to garage sales with my friends and family. One Friday night, I drove down to Seattle to spend the weekend with my good friend Melanie. We have been friends through thick and thin starting in sixth grade. She, along with my sister, was maid of honor at my wedding.

We celebrated our birthdays at the Newcastle golf course outside of Seattle on Friday night and then on Saturday morning we went to garage sales. The first one we went to was a fund raiser for a high school. The people working the sale were all parents. We asked them where all the students were and they looked at us like, "You've got to be kidding." They explained to us, "High school students are in bed at 8 AM on a Saturday morning." While the high school sale didn't have any actual high school students, it did have two little bikes for sale, one for a girl and one for a boy. They were the perfect sizes for my kids. The bikes even came with helmets. $5 for both! I couldn't have shipped our bikes up to Bellingham for that. What a bargain! My kids rode them all summer and I definitely got my money's worth.

Later that morning at a charity sale in a big barn in Issaquah we found a lot of neat things. Melanie spotted this American Tourister luggage set in purple that had been marked $20. The price had been slashed to $10 and I bought it. All this stuff fit in Melanie's huge rental car, but packing it all into my red Hyundai rental for the trip back to Bellingham was tricky. I have got to buy a truck.

I split the luggage set up, thinking that I would get the most money that way. The four pieces ended up selling for a total of $70.99 and went to three different states: Florida, North Carolina, and California. The piece that sold for the most was the train case for $20.50—it was darling. It was such a neat set that I thought my mother was going to try to keep it. She seems to collect luggage and she loves purple. We were living with her for the summer at her home on the edge of the San Juan Islands. Not a bad life!

#87 Orange Blossom Flatware

$15.00
Paid
From: Goodwill
San Diego, CA

Wm Rogers 1910 Art Nouveau 6 Teaspoons—OLD!

Description:
We have a lot of this silverplate flatware for sale. It is marked "Wm Rogers & Son AA Pat. Nov 29 1910." It is a lovely, heavily embossed art nouveau floral pattern. It may be the orange blossom pattern. If anyone knows we would appreciate knowing. I don't know how these pieces will polish up and they all have scratches from an overzealous polisher. These scratches may come out with good old-fashioned elbow grease. This auction is for 6 dinner forks which measure 7 5/8".

Winning Bid:

$116.53/8

Ended: 8/8/03
History: 26 bids for 8 auctions
Starting Bid: $9.99 each
Winner: DE, NV, CA, LA, OK

Viewed
000124 X

Orange Blossom Flatware   #87

The Story

Of the three main thrift store chains (Salvation Army, Value Village, and Goodwill), Goodwill is my hands-down favorite. They price fairly and move tons of merchandise. I have found that the Goodwill stores in the Los Angeles area are not great but the ones in San Diego are. I had to fly back down to California for a week during the summer to teach two Learning Annex classes, so while I was in San Diego I hit the Goodwill stores.

You will usually pay more for things in a thrift store than you would at a tag sale or garage sale, but that doesn't mean you can't find good values. I found a shopping cart full at one of the San Diego Goodwills before teaching my class. One of the items I picked up was this set of flatware in their boutique area. It was really art nouveau and even with the scratches, it was a lovely set.

I hadn't tried any flatware up to that point and thought I would give it a shot. I like multiple items in the same line—like dinnerware—because they are easier and quicker to list. People will most likely buy more than one item in your series and this helps increase the bid amounts. Flatware is also non-breakable (a very good thing) and quite easy to ship. I got 25 pieces in this pattern and I made them into eight auctions.

There was no pattern name on this set so I looked up flatware by William Rogers on eBay. I thought that it might be the Orange Blossom pattern, which is what I put in the auction description. Immediately after the auction started, I got an email from the nicest lady in Reno, Nevada. She said:

You are correct in your guess that this is the Orange Blossom pattern. In the early 1900's, each piece of store-bought citrus was wrapped in a piece of tissue with the Sunkist logo. Homemakers would collect the tissues and mail them to Sunkist with a few cents (much like Betty Crocker coupons) for various pieces of Orange Blossom Silverplate. A fork could be had for 24 wrappers plus 25 cents. The large ladle took 144 wrappers and $1.40. In 1993, Sunkist commissioned replicas of this beautiful pattern to celebrate its Centennial Anniversary. Yours, of course, are the original.
Susan (A Sunkist grower's daughter).

Goosebumps! She also faxed me pages of the different shapes the flatware was made in. eBayers are so nice! The eight auctions brought in $116.53 and the flatware went to five different states. As long as you can identify the pattern and you don't pay too much, flatware is the way to go!

#88 Carriage Lamp

Antique Iron Carriage Light/Lamp/Lantern—WOW!

Description:

Antique iron carriage light/lamp or lantern is 22" by 9" by 9". This piece is awesome. It is from the 1850's to 1890's, I am guessing. It is hand-made and a wonderful piece of architecture. It looks to be very gothic and heavy iron. It would make a great hanging lamp or large candle holder. It looks like it could have originally come from a church. It has a few dings otherwise in wonderful condition for its age. It is fantastic!

Winning Bid:

$78.⁸⁰

Ended: 8/13/03
History: 2 bids
Starting Bid: $49.99
Winner: N. Andover, MA

Viewed
`000045` X

Carriage Lamp #88

The Story

I wasn't able to go to garage sales every weekend while in Bellingham. I still had a lot of friends in the Northwest and it seemed like there were quite a few weekends that I had to attend functions like Zac's bar mitzvah and a high school girl's weekend away. To find enough things to sell, I spent a lot of time in the Bellingham Goodwill.

It was a great store. They put out new merchandise daily, took the American Express card (my card of choice), and even took returns within seven days on certain items! I started running into a lot of the same people, who included several antiques dealers, on my visits. I quickly learned that to find great items, you needed to check in on a regular basis. I used to go there at least every other day.

I also learned to make friends with the people who put out the merchandise. One day, I heard a Goodwill employee say to a dealer I knew, "Hey, Gary, I know that you look for lamp shades. Is this something you would like?" He held up a lamp shade that hadn't even been put on the shelf yet!

My grandmother often said, "You get more flies with honey than you do with vinegar." It still holds true.

I saw this carriage lamp on one of my visits and it was on a cart waiting to be put out. Goodwill policy frowned on buyers taking things from the carts and tubs themselves, so I waited for the employee to place it on the shelf. Then I grabbed it. Considering my background, which is heavy in lighting, my excitement about this unusual lantern is understandable. It was gorgeous and only $2.99.

The lantern was hand-made and unique. With no markings to guide me, I couldn't find out anything much about it in my research. It was heavy iron and I thought I should start the bidding at $49.99. That was a good move because it only got two bids and ended up selling for $78.80 to an antiques dealer in Massachusetts. As my grandmother used to say, "Sell for gain." I definitely did on that day.

#89 Amethyst Ring

$15.00
Shop Paid
From: Inheritance

Amethyst 14k Gold Diamond Tearshaped Ring—WOW

Description:
Beautiful tear drop shaped amethyst ring is 14k gold and also has 2 side diamonds. The size is 5/8" in diameter. This ring has been checked by my GIA (Gemological Institute of America) certified Brother

Winning Bid:

$26.00
Ended: 8/13/03
History: 2 bids
Starting Bid: $24.99
Winner: Ligonier, PA

Viewed
 000040 X

The Story

The girls who worked in the shop over the years were fantastic and have become my good friends. We always had a lot of fun but the cost of doing business when you have an actual retail location is quite high. There is so much overhead: rent, advertising and marketing expenses, employee salaries, inventory costs, bags, tissue, price tags, heat, electricity, and the list goes on. In addition, there is always the possibility of theft and breakage. You must also keep set hours and be open to serve your public. With eBay, a lot of these expenses and restrictions disappear. eBay enabled us to continue the business without an actual brick and mortar location.

In July of 2002, the last month my grandma's shop was open, a customer walked out with a tray of amethyst rings. There were 36 rings in the tray, or about $10,000 worth. That was it for me. It made my decision to close the business even easier.

About three months ago, I got a letter from the Bellingham Police Department saying that they had recovered some of the items from that theft. Four of the 36 rings had been traded to an undercover agent for drugs. Lovely.

My dad picked up the rings for me and I got them from him over the summer. Funny how there were four. I gave one to my brother, one to my mom, one to my sister, and I kept one for myself. I said to everyone, "Grandma—the gift that keeps on giving."

Amethyst is the birthstone for February. It's one of the more popular gemstones because of its rich, wine-like color. The color purple has traditionally been the color of royalty, and amethyst has been used for centuries to adorn monarchs and rulers. In terms of its composition, however, amethyst is simply a purple variety of quartz, which means that it's pretty affordable. I should have put all that in my listing!

I put my ring on eBay and started it at $24.99. This ring was priced at $135 in the shop. The secondary market for 14-carat gold and gemstones is not great. I was happy to get $26 for this darling ring. What a history it has! If only it could talk.

#90 Fukagawa Vase

$5.00
Paid

From: Goodwill
Bellingham, WA

Large Fukagawa Imari Grape Vase—Arita—AMAZING

Description:

This is a lovely and large grape Fukagawa vase. It is simply divine. It is 12" by 5 1/2". The colors are wonderful and include blue, blue purple, and rose/plum on a white porcelain. It is in excellent condition. The label says "Fukagawa Arita Japan" and "Purveyors to the Imperial Empire." I would date this piece from 1960-1980. It has the traditional Fukagawa mountain and river mark on the sticker and also in blue ink on the base.

Winning Bid: **$105.50**

Ended: 8/13/03
History: 3 bids
Starting Bid: $99
Winner: Covington, GA

Viewed
`000085` X

Fukagawa Vase #90

The Story

It was the summer of 2003 and I had been back in Bellingham for about a month. I could not bring myself to drive by my grandma's house and the old shop. I was having a hard time finding a place to work with fast and reliable internet access. One day I stopped by my dad's to plug in to his DSL and I spilled a Diet Coke all over my laptop. It stopped working. Things were going from bad to worse.

I decided I might as well make it even worse and drive by the shop. It was so sad. The house was all empty and looked gutted. Someone was taking down our Christmas lights from the front picket fence. The shop had been painted brown from 1969 until 1998. My grandma and I had decided that white would be a nice change and we had it painted white with a periwinkle blue trim in 1998. We even added a white picket fence around the front. It was so cute.

After driving by the store I figured I might as well get it all over with and head out to the mausoleum where my grandmother is buried. I had called my sister several days before and said, "Do you know what day it is?" She said, "I didn't but I do now. Thanks a lot." It was August 3, 2003—already three years since she had gone. Somehow facing the shop and the mausoleum wasn't as hard as I had thought it would be. Of course I cried, but it was almost easier than using all that energy to avoid them.

After visiting the mausoleum, I decided to cheer myself up by going to the Goodwill and poking around. I wandered over to the vase section and in with the clear flower vases I found this beautiful Japanese vase. It was signed with the original paper label—always good. It was $5, so I bought it.

Porcelain, a white-based clay, was developed in China by the fourth or fifth century. It was not until the seventeenth century that Japan began producing its own porcelain. In 1894, Chuji Fukagawa founded Fukagawa Porcelain with the goal of becoming world-renowned in artistic porcelain. He achieved his goal and his company has supplied porcelain to the Imperial Household of Japan since 1910. Its production processes are shaped by the belief that porcelain needs to be fired at high temperatures in order to ensure its strength.

When I got home and did my research, I found that Fukagawa pieces go for quite a bit. I started the bidding at $99 and was very happy with a selling price of $105.50. "Any old port in a storm," my grandma always said. The Goodwill was my port that day. P.S. My laptop dried out and started working again, too!

#91 Umpire Chest Plate

$?.00
Paid

From: Goodwill
Bellingham, WA

MacGregor B79 Umpire Chest Plate—Mens?—Mint

Description:

MacGregor Taiwan B-79 Umpire Chest plate is in excellent condition and almost looks brand new. It is a men's size and I am guessing that it would be a men's size medium or small. The dimensions are 22" by 24".

Winning Bid:

$15.51

Ended: 8/26/03
History: 5 bids
Starting Bid: $9.99
Winner: Norton, OH

Viewed

 **X**

Umpire Chest Plate #91

The Story

My six year old son played baseball for Palm Desert in the spring of 2003. The city of Palm Desert goes all out—huge fields with lights at night and snack bars that sell almost anything you can imagine. It was a far cry from T-ball in Bellingham. We felt like we were in the major leagues. My son got the baseball bug. Within four months (partly because of birthday gifts), he had four mitts, five bats, three pairs of baseball pants and had gone through about a hundred balls. He played in a summer league in Bellingham while we were there. He was obsessed!

He decided that he really needed some catcher's gear. He had received some money from his dad for his birthday so I said we could look on eBay. We found the greatest set of kid's gear—a mask, knee guards and a chest plate. I was bidding against a new eBayer with a big zero feedback by his name so I knew that he wouldn't know about sniping. The bidding was at $46. I placed a snipe bid for $58 max and waited. We won the auction for $55. The gear came and Houston was so excited.

About two weeks later I was in the Bellingham Goodwill and spotted another set of catcher's gear in the sporting section. When you're at a thrift store, don't just check one section—make sure you look everywhere. The set included a chest plate, mask and knee guards and was priced at $19.95. I also found one of those really thick chest plates that the umpires wear for $2.99. I bought it all.

I got the goods home and my seven-year-old told me that it was not catcher's gear but umpire gear. Oh boy. He tried it on and decided that he liked the mask and knee guards way better than the ones in the $55 set we just got. He said, "Please don't sell them on eBay." I said, "Okay, as long as you pay me the $20." He said, "Okay" and handed me all the money he had, $13. I decided to sell the extra chest plate on eBay. Houston looked at me and said, "Mommy, whatever it sells for you have to deduct from my purchase price of $20." I said, "Are you for real?" He is a businessman through and through.

We put it on eBay and I couldn't believe when it sold for almost $16. The rest of the set only cost my son $4.44—a lot cheaper than the first set we had bought.

#92 Leica Projector

Leitz/Leica Pradovit 253 IR Slide Projector

Description:

Leitz/Leica Pradovit 253 IR Projector. Excellent Condition, in box, missing slide tray. Originally $600. Box is 16 ½ by 12 ½ by 6 ½". Comes with remote! Specs: Low voltage (24V) quartz halogen lamp with low heat/light ratio; just under 1000 lumen; dual channel cooling; cast aluminum chassis, lamp housing cover, metal lens barrel; plastic lens mount.

Winning Bid: **$170.00**

Ended: 8/27/03
History: 7 bids
Starting Bid: $99
Winner: Nashua, NH

Viewed
000196 X

The Story

I had found this slide projector at my favorite thrift store. It was MIB (mint in box) and looked brand new. It still had the original price tag of $600 on it. It was priced at the thrift store for $5, so I grabbed it. You can't go wrong with items that are mint in the original box. Sometimes even empty antique boxes sell on their own. I read an article once about an empty antique tinker toy box that went for $70. Don't throw anything away. Have I said that recently?

I did my research and found that Leica products sell for quite a bit. Leica products enjoy an almost cult status. The Leica web site has this to say about the allure of its products:

On one hand they are highly refined designs that are fabricated with precision. On the other hand, they have an extraordinary aura that can evoke feelings and emotions. And it is precisely this unique combination of that warm aura and bold, perfect technology that created the Leica mystique.

Wow—I should have put all that in my listing. Leica is also famous for its association with inventor Oskar Barnack, who in 1914 was the first to take photos with a 35mm camera (which he had designed)—an impressive history and company.

When I put this slide projector up on eBay my brother called me and said, "Where did you get that?"

I told him it had come from my favorite thrift store and he said, "If it doesn't sell, I want to buy it." I let him know that, based on my research, it was probably going to sell for over my starting bid price of $99 and he said he didn't want it that badly. My brother is an amazing photographer and graphic artist. He did the layout and art for this book!

The projector sold in July for $182.50 while I was in Spain, but the winning bidder never paid. This does happen. We emailed the bidder three times over three weeks and received no response. We usually wait about a month and then we relist the item.

I relisted it from Bellingham this summer and it sold the second time for a little less, $170. This time the gentleman paid. That was more like it.

#93 North Carolina Jug

North Carolina Pottery Stoneware JUG—Signed!

Description:

Beautiful 3-sided North Carolina jug is 8 ½" by 4 ½". It has a wood stopper and I don't know if this is original or not. It is stoneware and in excellent condition. Could date anywhere from the 1890's to 1950's. It is signed/stamped "North Carolina." If anyone knows the maker or dating we would appreciate knowing. It has a wonderful glaze color and has a hint of blue throughout. A super piece.

Winning Bid:

$610.00

Ended: 9/1/03
History: 13 bids
Starting Bid: $99
Winner: Greenville, SC

Viewed
000584 X

North Carolina Jug #93

The Story

I was still in Bellingham when we started seeing advertisements for a huge charity sale. My mom and I arrived right on time and paid $10 each to get in an hour early. It was crazy. They even had shopping carts. I saw this jug and turned it over and it said North Carolina on the base. I had just done some research on North Carolina pottery and I remembered it was pretty good.

The place was filled with other antiques dealers. One of my dealer friends said, "How do you like California?" I said, "I love it. I can find $4 vases that turn into $400. I haven't found anything like that up here this summer." Little did I know that I had found something even better and it was already in my cart! At the checkout counter I found that the jug was going to cost $5. I asked my mom if I should get it and she said, "No way. That is too much money." I decided to try it anyway.

I was at Kinko's listing auctions and I put this one on with a starting price of $99 and a plea for help. Every hour when I am listing as a little treat I let myself check my auction totals. My totals jumped way up in a little over an hour. I checked the auction detail and found that it was due to the jug. I had listed it at 1:23 p.m. and by 3:10 p.m. it was up to $375. I had a winner! I called my mom to tell her and she said, "Never listen to your mother."

A nice eBayer emailed this information that I added to the listing:

This is the mark of Sam Propst (1882 to 1935). This piece is early 1930's, in a style called "swirl." According to *Maine Antique Digest*, 'Art pottery was a way for North Carolina potter-farmers to continue making a living after refrigeration and Pyrex nearly wiped out the utilitarian pottery market. Swirl, a side-by-side diagonal layering of light and dark clay throughout the body of a piece, had no practical purpose; it was devised by Sam Propst in the early 1930's, and when it sold, he continued making it.'

The jug ended up selling for $610. The buyer emailed me:

Received the pinch bottle and am quite pleased. Paid about top retail, but was persuaded by your description that it would be exceptional and it is. The blue is caused by traces of ore that sporadically appear in firing this local clay of Catawba Valley, NC. The potter never knows what the end result might be. Sometimes the blue really adds an extra appeal as in this case. A keeper!

#94 Tole Tray

Free
Paid
From: Charity sale
Bellingham, WA

Hand Painted Tole Tray—Floral Roses—Toleware!

Description:
Beautiful hand painted tole tray is black metal and the rose floral pattern is just lovely. It is done in blues, greens, purples, pinks and yellows. It has some slight bends, marks and is missing a little black on the edge. In overall great condition for its age. A vintage piece, 17" by 14".

Winning Bid: **$51.**⁰⁰

Ended: 9/1/03
History: 24 bids
Starting Bid: $9.99
Winner: Auburn, AL

Viewed
 **X**

Tole Tray #94

The Story

I got cartloads of really great things at the charity sale where I picked up the jug. As I was shopping, a woman stopped me and said "You are that eBay lady. I just sold your videos at online auction this week." I said, "Good for you. How much did you get?" She said "$28." "Not bad," I replied. As I was checking out to pay the second time, the ladies taking my money said, "You sure have a great eye." I said, "My grandmother had an antiques store for 52 years." In unison, the ladies said, "We know, we know—Cheryl Leaf Antiques." I forgot that I was back home.

After we thought we had everything in my shopping cart added up the second time around, one of the checkers said "Oops, we forgot that tray in the bottom." I asked, "How much?" She said, "You have been such a great customer—it's a free bonus." I need to attend a sale like this every week. Too bad they only come around once a summer!

I got the tole tray home along with all my other things and started in on my research. I discovered that I needed to say "toleware" in the auction title in addition to "tole painting." I think the fact that I included both terms is one reason the auction went so high and had 24 bids! I knew that tole painting was collectible, but I didn't realize how collectible.

Toleware was originally a French term meaning "sheet iron." The term now refers to hand painted decorated metal items, most notably tin. It is a form of folk art. The term folk art usually refers to art that gets used somehow rather than simply looked at. A tole-painted ash bucket, for example, would have been made for cleaning out the hearth, not simply for adorning it. The New England area is most well known for toleware. Toleware started to get popular in about 1800, and after 1850 many of the toleware pieces were stenciled rather than free form. Geometric designs, scenery, florals and fruits were all common decorations.

This tray sold for $51. Not bad for a free item! What kind of an ROI (return on investment) does that work out to? They didn't teach me that one in business school.

Sun., Oct. 21, 1951

Cheryl Leaf
ANTIQUES
and
GIFTS
2828 N. W. Ave.
Come in and Browse around!

#95 Antique Baroque Stainless

$3.00
Paid
From: Garage Sale
Bellingham, WA

Antique Baroque Wallace—7 Teaspoons—NICE

Description:

We have a lot of this stainless flatware up for auction this week. It is all signed "Wallace Silversmiths Korea 18/8" and the ornate pattern is called "Antique Baroque." The pieces are all in very good to excellent condition with some slight scratches. It all needs a good cleaning. This auction is for 7 teaspoons which measure 6" each.

Winning Bid:

$101.^{71}/6

Ended: 9/4/03
History: 29 bids for 6 auctions
Starting Bid: $9.99 each
Winner: Houston, TX
Phoenix, AZ

Viewed
000166 X

Antique Baroque Stainless   #95

The Story

My mom and I went to a strange garage sale out in the county surrounding Bellingham one Saturday. There were a lot of really expensive items and the guy looked familiar. I thought he might have been a dealer and my mom thought that maybe everything was stolen. My grandmother would have disagreed and said, "Always look for the best in others—not the worst." Anyway, his prices were too high on most things. I had been successful with silverplated flatware, so I thought I would try some stainless. This was a pretty pattern and he only wanted $3 for 34 pieces so I bought it.

When I got divorced three years ago, I needed babysitting help at night. I placed an ad with the local college and one of the first girls I met was Brianne Smith. She was perfect. When I was interviewing her she mentioned that she had been a camp counselor at Camp Sealth outside of Seattle. I had goosebumps. My grandmother had spent many summers at the Campfire Girl's Camp Sealth. She was hired! Brianne became part of our family and she helped me this summer with eBay.

Before selling any flatware you must identify the pattern. This can take hours. Luckily, Brianne was there and I asked her to look on eBay and a few other popular flatware web sites. Sometimes you get lucky and other times you can waste an afternoon. She ended up finding this one right away, mostly because the patterns were all alphabetized by manufacturer and then by pattern name, and this one was called "Antique Baroque." Yipppeee!

There are three main types of flatware. They are stainless, silverplate and sterling silver. Stainless is made of metal that has been coated with any of a number of finishes to resist stain or corrosion. Silverplate is the same thing, but coated in silver. Sterling silver is made of an alloy that is 92.5% silver and 7.5% another metal, typically copper. Sterling flatware, often called "silverware," is usually marked either "sterling" or ".925."

I divided up the flatware into six different auctions. I did two serving spoons, five salad forks, seven dinner forks, seven teaspoons, six tablespoons, and seven knives. The auction that sold for the most was the seven teaspoons for $22.01. All six of the auctions added up to $101.71. Not bad! Brianne couldn't believe how much it all sold for. She has dabbled in eBay and is thinking about selling again to help supplement the cost of her graduate school studies in audiology. Don't throw away that drawer full in the kitchen just yet!

#96 Ping Zing Golf Grips

14 Ping Zing Golf Club Grips—Karsten Dyla—WOW

Description:

14 Ping Zing Golf Club Grips are marked "Karsten Dyla Grip."
They are 11" long. I can't tell if they are new or used. They look
new on the ends. There are little brown specks in the black areas
and I guess these are part of the design. Marked "Golf pride USA
pat 5087042." Whether new or used, they look in good condition
to me.

Winning Bid:

$45.71

Ended: 9/11/03
History: 21 bids
Starting Bid: $9.99
Winner: Spring Lake, MI

Viewed
000397 X

Ping Zing Golf Grips #96

The Story

We were back in California just in time for the school year to start. I had just taught my very last Learning Annex classes in San Diego and Los Angeles. I admit I was a little sad. Those classes were a great forum for me to help others and a great way for me to get to tell my stories. It was in my last class that the "goosebumps" comment about the mourning hair piece gave me the inspiration to tell my stories to a larger audience. My grandmother would have said, "Everything happens for a reason." It was time for me to move on.

I was out on Saturday morning doing my garage sale route and following my map when I decided to go over to the Goodwill. On my way back from the Goodwill I saw a sign for a garage sale in a city I don't typically shop. I was never one of those "I brake for garage sales!" types, but I guess I am now. How embarrassing!

I always try to buy one thing at every garage sale. I force myself to find one item of redeeming value. I always say hello, goodbye, and thanks when I go to garage sales. My family taught me good manners. Buying one thing also makes the seller feel better, and you may be helping them more than you know. When people used to come into the shop needing to sell things to buy food for their kids or gas for their cars, my grandma always figured out a way to get them money without compromising their dignity. Even if the item they were offering was not worth anything, she would ask me to go and get ten or twenty dollars from the other room. I didn't understand it then, but I do now.

These golf club grips were the one thing I found during this unscheduled stop. I asked how much, and they wanted fifty cents each. I said, "How much if I buy them all?" Two dollars, they said. Sold! I knew that Ping was a good company. As a wedding gift, I had bought my ex-husband Ping Zing golf clubs. They set me back about $700.

Ping was founded by a Norwegian named Karsten Solheim, who was 42 when he first started to play golf. Six years later, at 48, he invented his first putter in his garage in Redwood, City California. His background was in engineering, and he applied basic engineering principles to his putter. He named it "Ping" because of the sound it made when it struck a golf ball. He began manufacturing his putters in that same garage in 1959, and the rest is history. His company is a great testament to finding your passion a little later in life!

I put these grips on with a starting bid of $9.99. We had lots of inquiries, and 397 people looked at this auction. Ping has a tremendous following. My $2 item sold for $45.71!

I Brake for Garage Sales

#97   700 Match Books

$10.^**00**
Paid

From: Estate Sale, Palm Desert, CA

LOT 100 Matches/Match Books—Vintage CA/NV #1

Description:

We recently bought a super collection of matches/match books. Most still have all the matches in them and have not even been used—in very good to excellent condition. They are vintage from the 1950's to present. Mostly they are from hotels, airlines and restaurants. A lot are from the LA Area. This is lot #3 and contains 100 match books. A few of the areas the matches are from include: Hong Kong, Los Angeles, Palm Springs, Northern California/San Francisco. Even includes matches from the now-defunct PSA Airlines.

Winning Bid:

$80.^**05**/**7**

Ended: 9/20/03
History: 17 bids for 7 auctions
Starting Bid: $9.99
Winner: Paris, WA, FL, LA

Viewed

000437 X

The Story

I went to an estate sale and saw the coolest huge brandy sifter. I knew that bar ware does very well on eBay and I thought I would see how much it was. It was filled with match books. My grandmother had always kept match books in a very rare antique cloisonné bowl on her hearth. I have the match books and rare bowl on the hearth in my office today.

The seller wanted $10 for everything. I bought it and hauled it out to my car. A gentleman saw my car filled to the brim and said "Haven't you done enough damage today?" "Almost," I replied. I could still stick a few more things in around the edges. I called my brother the other day and mentioned that I am going to buy a cheap used truck soon and he said, "Your car will thank you." He is right.

I put the large brandy sifter on eBay right away for $24.99. Didn't sell. Relisted it at $9.99. Didn't sell. Relisted it a third time at $4.99. Didn't sell. It now sits on that lower part of the same hearth in my office and serves as Mari's packing garbage can. I make mistakes all the time! Luckily I still had the matches. I figured that there were 700 of them and I decided to put

them on in seven different lots of one hundred each.

They ended up selling to WA, FL, and LA, and four lots even went to Paris, France. Here is the email from Monique in Paris:

Hello, I have received yesterday your matches and I spent a wonderful evening looking at them. Thanks a lot. I'm very happy. Have a nice day.

"How romantic!" my kids would say. They say it all the time and they have no idea what it means.

#98 Eames Bubble Lamp

$20.⁰⁰

Paid

From: Estate sale
Palm Desert, CA

George Nelson/Howard Miller Bubble Lamp—Disc!

Description:
Super neat bubble lamp is in the saucer or disc shape. It is about
7" by 19". It has the original label which says "Bubble Lighting
Fixtures Patent applied for Zeeland MI Bubble inc." Zeeland MI
is the home of the Howard Miller Clock Company, which made
these lamps from a George Nelson design from 1947 until 1979.
It works and is so cool! It is in very good condition with about 3-4
tiny pushed-in places.

Winning Bid: **$231.⁰⁰**

Ended: 9/24/03
History: 19 bids
Starting Bid: $99
Winner: Los Angeles, CA

Viewed
000349 X

Eames Bubble Lamp   #98

The Story

When I was twelve years old I had a cocker spaniel named Rollo. One day we found that Rollo had cancer and was going to have to be put to sleep. I was devastated for about a month. My grandmother couldn't bear to see me like that so she said, "Would $200 buy you a nice new puppy?" You bet it would. Off we went to a top cocker spaniel breeder in Onalaska, WA, and I picked out "John," later to be dubbed "Springdale Buffington." We called him Buffy.

He was an AKC registered show dog and I started to show him professionally. I was only 12 years old and yet I was competing against professional handlers. My dad would drive me to Canada to show Buffy on weekends. Buffy's father, "Wynden's Weird Harold," had been a champion, and I wanted to make Buffy one also. It takes fifteen points in Canada to become a champion. Each time you win a best-in-class, you get a certain amount of points towards your dog's championship. Buffy had about twelve points when I decided I would rather focus on high school. It was too bad, but I learned a lot from competing—like how to be tough and how to win and lose graciously.

It is a competitive world and garage sales are no exception. I arrived at an estate sale in Palm Desert right when it opened. The ad read "Estate Priced to Move." People were already carrying boxes out when I got there. Everything was Eames-era, mid-century modern. I found a yellow metal bubble lamp for $15 and a bunch of other neat things. I dumped the things I was planning to buy in a pile in one of the rooms. I came back to find another dealer going through

it. I said "Those are mine." He explained to me that in this competitive market you had better carry everything around with you, or someone else will take it.

As I was leaving, the nice gentleman running the sale said, "Hey, you like lamps. How about this one?" It was hanging over the dining room table and I hadn't even noticed it. It was marked $25 and I offered $20. Done deal.

The white bubble lamp turned out to be an authentic George Nelson design for the Howard Miller Clock Company. The original lamps were only made from 1947 until 1979. Modernica is currently reproducing them, but my lamp had the original sticker from Miller. George Nelson was an architect by trade. He is famous for his modern classic design and modular office furniture.

The yellow metal lamp I picked out only sold for $9.99 and the one the gentleman talked me into went for $231! He really was a gentleman and you just never know what something is worth until you sell it!

#99 Dive Watch

$51.⁰⁰

Peter Paid

From: Peter
A gift

Invicta MIB Blue Ladies' Dive/Diver Watch—$200 MSRP

Description:
NEW Ladies' Invicta Blue Divers Watch Model #9177 (Retail:
$200). This reliable and sporty Invicta dive watch displays the
date and time in solid stainless steel construction and is water-re-
sistant to 200 meters (660 ft.). Topped with a rotating blue diver's
bezel, you won't find a better timepiece for the job or the price.
This is a BRAND NEW, never worn, genuine Invicta watch.

**Winning
Bid:**

$76.⁰⁰

Ended: 9/26/03
History: 6 bids
Starting Bid: $49.99
Winner: Jupiter, FL

Viewed
000112 X

The Story

My good friend Peter Gineris is a scuba diver. I have gone on several diving trips with him and because I am terrified of scuba diving I stay on the boat and watch. In San Diego this January at the Lobster Shack, I actually put on a wet suit. I had planned to snorkel with the sea lions, but was having second thoughts when the dive master pushed me in. The shock of being pushed in took my breath away. I managed to stay in for about twenty minutes because the sea lions were so cute. I was starting to see the appeal of scuba.

This past May I decided to face my fears. I took a class from Kathy Pepper, owner of "Get Wet Scuba" in Palm Springs. The class was fun and interesting. The first day at the pool with all our gear on was a different story. We had to drop to our knees and stay underwater to start learning skills. I freaked out but somehow kept myself in the water.

The next pool session was at night, and all eight of us were going into the fifteen-foot deep end. I said "Kathy, I can't do it. I have to leave." She said "Why?" She explained to me that she had never seen fear in my eyes. She has been teaching for a long time and knows when someone is afraid. She said, "You have never been afraid." Wow! I started to believe in myself. I still left that night but decided to finish in private pool sessions.

The private pool time was just what I needed. I passed the class! It took me until September to attempt the open water. On the last day at Catalina Island, I almost lost it when I had to remove my mask in cold water and sit for one minute without it on the bottom of the ocean. Then I had to put the mask back on and clear out the water. I was determined to pass and I succeeded!

Peter sent me this scuba watch as a gift. It was a women's watch, but I really like a larger face. He had bought it on eBay and I asked if it was okay for me to sell it and get a men's version. No problem. He had paid $51. When I put it back on eBay I put the $200 MSRP (Manufacturer's Suggested Retail Price from their web site) in the title. I think it helped. The watch (almost sold for $76—$25 50%) more than he had paid on eBay a few weeks before. Hmmmm!

#100 Queen Anne Canapé

$1.00 Paid

From: Garage sale Palm Desert, CA

Queen Anne Silver Folding Canapé Tray—AWESOME

Description:
This is so cute. It is marked "Queen Anne Made in England Silver-Plated." It is a folding serving or canapé tray. It has three 7 1/4" round serving plates and is 9 3/4" tall. Too awesome! Very slight wear and some minor scratches, overall in excellent condition. I see no pitting or tarnish problems.

Winning Bid:

$86.00

Ended: 10/8/03
History: 22 bids
Starting Bid: $9.99
Winner: Seattle, WA

Viewed

000055 X

Queen Anne Canapé #100

The Story

This is the last story in my book and I don't want it to end. I loved writing this book. I had laughs, tears, remembrances and joy every day during this process. I said to my mom, "I don't want to finish this book." She said, "Start writing the next one." My first thought was, I wrote this one in two months. I need a break. My friend Peter offered this insight: "When you really love a character you are writing about, that is all you think about when living your life." Wow! He was right. I really loved my main character, Cheryl Leaf. Does anyone doubt that? I got to think about her everyday. It was wonderful.

Let's finish this book before I start on my next volume. So here goes. I was out doing the garage sales one Saturday and had my route planned. There was an unadvertised sale where I stopped. The woman holding the sale had great taste and all her things were wonderful. She had this folding silverplated serving tray and she only wanted $1. I bought it.

I got it home and did my research. There were only four items listed as Queen Anne silverplate and they did not sell for much. I never figured out if Queen Anne was the company or the pattern. I couldn't find the correct term for this tray so I made up my own, "Folding Canapé Tray." Canapé is a fancy term for an appetizer or hors d'oeuvre. My son Houston was in my office one day and he saw it and said, "Wow, Mommy, this is so cool. Can we keep it?" I said, "Houston, it is already listed on eBay. If it doesn't sell, then yes we can keep it. But otherwise, I will look for another." He was really intrigued with it. I think it was because he likes mechanical things and this was engineered so well.

When I tell him that we can keep something, he holds me to it. Once I had sold a railroad lantern on eBay. Houston saw it in my office and he made me promise that the next one would be his. Of course I forgot about it, but my seven-year-old didn't. I got another lantern about a month ago and it is now proudly displayed with his train things.

This tray really surprised me when it sold for $86. It was really beautiful. I told Houston I didn't know if we could afford to keep the next one we get. That is a lot of money!

Afterword

I've recorded all these stories as I've heard them told or lived them, and they are as accurate as I can remember. I had my mom, my dad, and my good friends Melanie and Peter as great readers to help me get the facts correct. My dad called me one day and said, "You say the semi-truck is 52' in one story and 54' in another. It was 53'." I said, "No, no, no—it was an even number. Can you please call and verify with Ed at Ludtke Trucking?" My dad gruffly agreed. As soon as I hung up the phone and before he verified it, I went in to my files and changed all the truck references to 53'. My dad is always right, but I had to give him a hard time.

The history and background of particular antiques, styles, and companies were drawn from my grandmother's notes, things I remembered, the internet, and multiple reference books. I never based a summary on just one source, so I didn't make any specific attributions in the book. I do not guarantee any facts, but I did my due diligence to double-check everything.

I also had my fantastic brother, Lee Dralle, and wonderful Becky Raney at *Print & Copy* in Bellingham to work with on the creative end. It was tough going at first, but we really got it figured out and I think the layout is fantastic. My editor, Susan Thornberg, was brilliant at making my voice come through loud and clear. I had a great team to work with and it was so much fun doing this book!

These are the first *100 Best*, and I hope to do a sequel of the second *100 Best*. I am also working on compiling a book about the 100 best things *you* all have sold on eBay and the 100 best things *you* all have bought on eBay. Please send or email me your great stories (AllAboard@mail.com)!

Writing this book was a journey. I hate to use an already-overused metaphor, but it fits. Remembering each story helped me work my way through the grief and pain I still feel at the loss of my grandmother. I cried almost every day I worked on this, and so did some of my friends and family. My mom called me one day, sobbing hysterically. I asked, "What's wrong?" and she blubbered out, "Number 34, the car." I knew how she felt. One day I was crying so hard when I was typing that I had to shut my eyes—but I kept on writing.

Grief and loss is something everyone can relate to. Working through it is a journey and this book helped me honor my grandmother and get a few more miles down the road. From the bottom of my heart, I thank you for reading it.

Order now from The Queen of Auctions:

 The 100 Best Things I've Sold on eBay—This paperback version— Makes a great gift ....$16.00 ea

 iBuy—A 3-ring loose-leaf binder system for tracking your online auction PURCHASES (200 pages w/tab dividers) .... $25.00 ea

 iSell—A 3-ring loose-leaf binder system for tracking your online auction SALES (200 pages w/tab dividers) .... $25.00 ea

 "Trash to Cash" Videos-Episodes 1 & 2—An instructional video set for doing garage sales and putting things up for sale at online auction. Watch how $74 turns into $569 in cyberspace on a Saturday morning with Lynn $30.00/both

 Set of 12 Greeting Cards— One each of 12 different styles-antique postcard art greeting cards w/coordinating designer envelopes. $40.00/set

Name_____

Address _____

City _____ State _____ Zip _____

Email_____ Telephone _____

$ _____   Items
$ _____   Media Mail Shipping ($3 for 1st item and $1 each additional)
$ _____   Sales Tax 7.75% CA Residents ONLY

$ _____   Total Enclosed

CHECKS Payable to:
All Aboard Inc.
PO Box 14103
Palm Desert, CA 92255

To **CHARGE** your order, please fill in the information below:
_____ American Express _____ Discover _____ Visa _____ Master Card

Account No. _____ Expiration_____

Signature_____

OR ORDER ONLINE at www.TheQueenOfAuctions.com or **FAX** (760) 345-9441